Preface

The decade of the 1960s was characterized by an explosion of human resources programs. One followed the other in rapid succession until nearly a score were devised to address the multiple manpower problems of the disadvantaged in the job market. During the 1970s, attention turned to the difficulties of assimilating these diverse manpower programs.

Paralleling these events was the development in the early 1960s of the revenue-sharing concept later adopted by the Nixon Administration as part of the proposed New Federalism.

Both developments--the perceived need for reforming the collection of manpower programs and the Administration's drive for revenue-sharing programs--led to the enactment of the Comprehensive Employment and Training Act of 1973--CETA (P. L. 93-203). This legislation, the first of a series of proposed special revenue-sharing bills, transferred control over a large portion of federal revenues to state and local jurisdictions for flexible use in lieu of a variety of categorical federal manpower programs.

The premises supporting decentralization and decategorization--the two basic tenets of CETA--are: 1) that local authorities know best local needs and how to respond to them, and 2) to deal effectively with those needs, maximum flexibility in the use of manpower resources should replace the present system of categorical programs.

To examine these premises and assess the social, economic, and political effects of this new approach to the delivery of manpower services, a Committee on Evaluation of Employment and Training Programs was established in the National Research Council early in 1974. The Committee's tasks are scheduled to be completed in 1977 and a final report to be published at that time. In the interim, however, several analytical papers will be prepared on specific facets of the transformation of a complex system of programs and relationships. This paper, prepared by the staff, is the first of such reports; it covers the early transition period of CETA.

The data for this study come primarily from a sample of 28 units of government that encompass all types of prime sponsors (six cities, nine counties, nine consortia, and four states). The sample has also been designed to represent variations in population and degree of unemployment (see Appendix B, Table 1, p. 146).

Twenty resident field research associates have been selected to follow the implementation and operation of CETA for three years in the 28 prime sponsor jurisdictions. Several interview waves are planned. This interim report summarizes the findings of the first phase of the study. The focus is on six substantive concerns in Title I (Comprehensive Manpower Services):

- Distribution of resources
- Planning process
- Administrative process
- Arrangements for delivering services to program clients
- Mix of manpower programs
- Type of people served

To obtain information the field research associates interviewed a minimum of seven key persons in each area representing officials responsible for implementing CETA as well as others with a more independent interest in manpower development. The research associates summarized and interpreted the formal interviews and supplemented them with additional information and insights. These 28 field research associate reports provided the basis for this study. The field work and much of the data used in preparing this interim report relate to the early transition period (January-April 1975). The findings should therefore be considered in relation to this time frame. For the same reasons, recommendations would be premature at this time.

Two unanticipated developments occurred shortly after CETA went into effect: the serious deterioration of the economy, and the enactment of the Emergency Jobs and Unemployment Assistance Act (EJUAA), which added Title VI (public service employment) to CETA. Both occurred too late to be reflected in the survey instruments. However, the research associates were able to address, if only marginally, the implications of these new events.

The evaluation study is part of the program of the Assembly of Behavioral and Social Sciences in the National Research Council. William Mirengoff, who originated the idea for the project, is the study director, and is assisted by Lester Rindler, senior research associate, and Richard C. Piper, research assistant. Marian D. Miller and Joyce E. Storms constitute the supporting staff.

I am grateful to the authors of this interim report and to members of the Committee on Evaluation of Employment and Training Programs, who conscientiously reviewed the successive drafts of the staff paper and provided advice and guidance during its development.

Many persons on Congressional staffs, in federal, state, and local governments, and in public interest groups have been consulted in the course of the study. The authors wish to acknowledge the cooperation of persons in the national and regional offices of the Department of Labor Manpower Administration who provided data and commented on draft materials.

The authors are particularly indebted to the resident field research associates whose expertise in public administration, manpower, economics, and education has

been a unique resource. Thanks are due to CETA
administrators and others who helped in the pretest of
the survey schedules in Alexandria, Va., Bucks County,
Pa., and in New York State, and to respondents in the
sample areas who gave generously of their time. The
authors are also grateful for the assistance of Betti
Goldwasser in selecting the survey sample and assembling historical data on funding and resource allocations,
and to Phyllis Groom McCreary and Christine L.
McShane, who edited the final document.

   This study was prepared under a grant from the
Ford Foundation.

Philip J. Rutledge, Chairman
Committee on Evaluation of
Employment and Training
Programs

Committee on Evaluation of Employment and Training Programs

Philip J. Rutledge, (Chairman), Director, Office of Policy Analysis, National League of Cities and U.S. Conference of Mayors

Curtis C. Aller, President, Center for Applied Manpower Research

Samuel Bernstein, Human Resources Director, Office of the Mayor, City of Chicago

Dorothy M. Burns, Acting President, Castleton State College

Philip E. Converse, Program Director, Institute for Social Research, University of Michigan

William L. Heartwell, Commissioner, Virginia Employment Commission

Paul Jennings, President, International Union of Electrical, Radio and Machine Workers

Gerald G. Somers, Professor of Economics, Department of Economics, University of Wisconsin

- - - - -

William Mirengoff, Project Director

Survey Areas and
Field Research Associates

Arizona:
  Phoenix-Maricopa Consortium
  Balance of Arizona
       Edmund V. Mech, Professor, Graduate School of
       Social Service Administration, Arizona State
       University

California:
  Long Beach
  Orange County Consortium
       Walter Fogel, Professor, Institute of Industrial
       Relations, University of California

  Stanislaus County
  San Joaquin Consortium
       John Mitchell, Research Associate, Center for
       Applied Manpower Research

Florida:
  Pasco County
  Pinellas County-St. Petersburg Consortium
       Emile Bie, formerly Deputy Director, Office of
       Technical Support, U. S. Employment Service

Illinois:
  Cook County
      Douglas Windham, Associate Professor, Depart-
      ment of Education, University of Chicago

Indiana:
  Gary
      William S. Griffith, Associate Professor, Depart-
      ment of Education, University of Chicago

Kansas:
  Topeka
      Charles Krider, Assistant Professor, School of
      Business, University of Kansas

  Kansas City/Wyandotte County Consortium
      Joseph Pichler, Dean, School of Business, Univer-
      sity of Kansas

Maine:
  Maine
      Roderick A. Forsgren, Professor and Associate
      Dean, Graduate School, University of Maine

Michigan:
  Calhoun County
      Earl Wright, Senior Staff Member, Upjohn Institute

  Lansing Tri-County Regional Manpower Consortium
      Michael Borus, Professor, School of Labor and
      Industrial Relations, Michigan State University

Minnesota:
  St. Paul
  Ramsey County
      James E. Jernberg, Associate Director for Adminis-
      tration, School of Public Affairs, University of
      Minnesota

New Jersey:
Middlesex County
Union County
    Jack Chernick, Professor, Institute of Management and Labor Relations, Rutgers University

New York:
New York City
    Lois Blume, Professor, New School for Social Research

North Carolina:
Raleigh Consortium
    Robert M. Fearn, Associate Professor, North Carolina State University

Balance of North Carolina
    Alvin M. Cruze, Manager, Human Resource Economics Department, Center for Resource Planning, Research Triangle Institute

Ohio:
Lorain County
    Jan Muczyk, Assistant Professor, Department of Management and Labor, Cleveland State University

Cleveland Western Reserve Manpower Consortium
    Robert N. Baird, Associate Professor, Department of Economics, Case Western Reserve University

Pennsylvania:
Philadelphia
Chester County
    David Zimmerman, Assistant Professor, Department of Management, Temple University

Texas:
Capital Area Consortium
Balance of Texas
    Lorna A. Monti, Research Associate, Bureau of Business Research, University of Texas

Contents

Chapter 1 Overview   1

   Introduction   1
   Extent of Decategorization and Decen-
      tralization   4
   CETA Planning: Expectations and Findings   7
   Administering Local Programs   9
   CETA Participants   11
   Effects of Decategorization   12
   Emerging Issues   13
   Summary   17

Chapter 2 Resources and Allocations   20

   Appropriations for Manpower Programs   20
   Title I Allocation Formula   25
   Measurement of Unemployment and Poverty   29
   Title II and Title VI Allocation Formulas   32
   Effect of Title I Formula   34
   Summary   44

Chapter 3 Manpower Planning   46

   Planning Before CETA   46
   The Geography of CETA Planning   49
   Planning Council Organization   50
   Composition of Local Planning Councils   52

Council Functions   56
Decision Making   58
Developing the Planning Document   61
State Planning   63
Summary   65

Chapter 4 The Administrative Process   67

Before CETA   68
Local Government Takes Over   71
Administrative Headaches   73
Elected Officials   76
The State's Role   78
Forming Consortia   82
The Regional Office Role   84
Summary   87

Chapter 5 The Delivery System   89

The Transition   92
Changing Institutions   94
Coordinating Manpower Services   98
The Employment Service   103
Public Vocational Education Institutions   108
Community-Based Organizations   112
Summary   117

Chapter 6 Program, Before and After   119

Estimates vs. Experience   120
Program Mix in Sample Areas   123
Summary   126

Chapter 7 The Participants   127

Number and Characteristics of Participants   128
Characteristics of Title I Participants by
  Type of Sponsor   133
Flow of Clients Through the System   136
Summary   138

Appendixes   141

    Appendix A List of Manpower Acronyms   141
    Appendix B Statistical Tables   145

Bibliography   171

Text Tables

    Table 1   Department of Labor Obligations
               for Work and Training Pro-
               grams, Fiscal Years 1963,
               1970-1975   21
    Table 2   Fiscal Year 1974 and Fiscal Year
               1975 Appropriations Com-
               parable Manpower Programs   23
    Table 3   Elements and Weights in CETA
               Allocation Formulas, Titles I,
               II, and VI   33
    Table 4   CETA Title I Funds Available
               and Allocated, Fiscal Year 1975   35
    Table 5   Percent Distribution of Manpower
               Funds, Fiscal Year 1974 and
               Fiscal Year 1975, by State
               Quintiles Based on Amount of
               Funds in Fiscal Year 1974   36
    Table 6   Percent Distribution and Relative
               Change of Manpower Funds,
               Fiscal Year 1974 and Fiscal
               Year 1975, by Region   37
    Table 7   Low Income Adults/Unemployment
               Ratio, by State Quintiles Based
               on Relative Change in Manpower
               Funds from Fiscal Year 1974 to
               Fiscal Year 1975, Title I   38
    Table 8   Percent Distribution of Manpower
               Funds, Fiscal Year 1974 and
               Fiscal Year 1975, by Type of
               Sponsor   39
    Table 9   Percent Fiscal Year 1975 of Fiscal
               Year 1974 Manpower Funds, by
               Type of Sponsor   40

Table 10   Percent Distribution Fiscal Year 1974 and Fiscal Year 1975 Manpower Funds Compared with Hypothetical Allocations, by Type of Sponsor   41

Table 11   Percent Distribution of Fiscal Year 1974 and Fiscal Year 1975 Manpower Funds by Component Sections of Minneapolis-St. Paul Standard Metropolitan Statistical Area   42

Table 12   Relationship of Sample Local Prime Sponsor Planning Structure to Pre-CETA Planning Structure   51

Table 13   Composition of Sample Local Prime Sponsor Planning Councils, Fiscal Year 1975, and Comparison with Pre-CETA Councils   54

Table 14   Composition of Sample Local Prime Sponsor Planning Councils, by Type of Sponsor, Fiscal Year 1975   56

Table 15   Disposition of Pre-CETA Manpower Programs Under CETA, by Type of Local Sponsor   96

Table 16   Selected Manpower Programs Operated by Local Sample Prime Sponsor Before CETA and Under CETA   97

Table 17   Funds and Local Manpower Projects of Community-Based Organizations, Fiscal Year 1974 and Fiscal Year 1975   113

Table 18   Percent Distribution of Planned and Actual Expenditures and Enrollments by Program Activity, CETA Title I, U. S. Totals, Fiscal Year 1975, and for Fiscal Year 1974 Comparable Programs   122

Table 19   Percent Distribution of Expendi-
           tures and Enrollments by
           Program Activity and by Type
           of Sponsor, CETA Title I
           Fiscal Year 1975 Sample Prime
           Sponsors   124

Table 20   Characteristics of CETA Title I
           Participants, U.S. Total,
           Second, Third, and Fourth
           Quarters, Fiscal Year 1975,
           Compared with Participants of
           Similar Categorical Programs,
           Fiscal Year 1974   132

Table 21   Characteristics of CETA Title I
           Participants, U.S. Total,
           by Type of Prime Sponsor,
           Second Quarter, Fiscal Year
           1975   134

Table 22   Characteristics of CETA Title I
           Participants, Sample Prime
           Sponsor Areas, Fiscal Year 1975   135

Appendix B Tables   145

Table 1   Selected Data for Sample Prime
           Sponsor Areas   146

Table 2   Federal Obligations for Work and
           Training Programs Administered
           by the Department of Labor,
           Selected Fiscal Years 1963-1974   149

Table 3   CETA Title II and Emergency
           Employment Act Allocations,
           Fiscal Year 1974, CETA Titles
           II and VI Allocations, Fiscal
           Year 1975, Sample Prime
           Sponsors   150

Table 4   CETA Title I Allocations Fiscal
           Year 1975 Sample Prime
           Sponsors   152

Table 5   CETA Title I Allocations, Fiscal
Year 1975, Compared with
Obligations for Comparable
Manpower Programs for Fiscal
Year 1974, by State   154

Table 6   Federal Obligations for Manpower
Programs, Total and Depart-
ment of Labor, Compared with
Gross National Product Fiscal
Years 1972-1976   156

Table 7   Federal Obligations and Partici-
pants, Manpower Programs
Corresponding with CETA
Title I, Fiscal Year 1974   157

Table 8   Planned and Actual Expenditures
by Program Activity, CETA
Title I, Fiscal Year 1975,
Sample Prime Sponsors   158

Table 9   Planned and Actual Enrollees by
Program Activity, CETA
Title I, Fiscal Year 1975,
Sample Prime Sponsors   162

Table 10   Characteristics of Participants
in CETA Title I, Fiscal Year
1975, Sample Prime Sponsors   166

Table 11   Characteristics of Participants
in CETA Titles I, II, and VI
Programs, Fiscal Year 1975,
Compared with Participants in
Similar Fiscal Year 1974
Programs   168

1
Overview

INTRODUCTION

The antecedents of manpower programs can be
traced to the 1930s and earlier, but the current emphasis dates from the Area Redevelopment Act of 1961 and
the Manpower Development and Training Act of 1962
(MDTA). Two distinct periods are identifiable: from
1963 to 1970, and from 1971 to the present. The earlier
period focused on structural problems in the labor
market--the intractable difficulties of the poor and disadvantaged who lacked the preparation, experience, and
skills to get and hold a job. New programs providing
remedial education, training, and work experience
would, it was hoped, enhance their employability.
These were authorized by the MDTA, the Economic
Opportunity Act (EOA), and civil rights legislation.
The economic setting was favorable; during most of the
period, employment demand was expanding. It was
possible to find jobs for some of the disadvantaged
workers in the interstices of the job market.

The current period, beginning in the early 1970s,
was marked by counter-cyclical programs in response
to rising unemployment levels. The Emergency Employment Act of 1971 (EEA), which subsidized state and
local public service jobs for a two-year period, was

1

designed to put unemployed people--not necessarily the
most disadvantaged--into employment quickly while
providing badly needed public services in local
communities.

By the end of the 1960s, there were more than 17
programs, each with its own legislative and organizational base, funding source, and regulations. Out of
these so-called categorical programs flowed 10,000 or
more specific manpower projects, often several in the
same community competing for the same clientele and
resources. These programs generally were conducted
through public and nonpublic agencies but not through
the local governments themselves.

Although there had been general dissatisfaction with
this patchwork approach for some time, it was not until
the end of 1973 that Congress and the Administration
agreed upon a manpower reform bill, and the Comprehensive Employment and Training Act (CETA) was
passed.

The new law, which became effective in July 1974,
transferred control of Department of Labor manpower
programs to state and local officials. Cities and counties of 100,000 or more (and combinations thereof) may
under Title I receive federal funds to develop and run
the types of manpower programs that they find most useful for their needs.[1]/

Major shifts in methods of delivering government
services occur infrequently, hence a study of the changes
resulting from CETA affords an opportunity to examine
the impact of such a major shift on human resources
programs. The central issue is the impact of decentralization and decategorization--the essential features of
CETA--on places, programs, and people, and on the
administration of manpower programs.

The confluence of several forces made the enactment of CETA in December 1973 possible. First,
Congress and federal manpower administrators were
convinced of the need to overhaul the burgeoning pro-
fusion of manpower programs. Second, the Nixon
Administration had embraced the New Federalism and

[1]/ See p. 3 for a summary of the act.

SUMMARY OF THE COMPREHENSIVE
EMPLOYMENT AND TRAINING ACT

The Comprehensive Employment and Training Act of 1973 (PL 93-203, as amended) has seven titles:

Title I establishes a program of financial assistance to state and local governments (prime sponsors) for comprehensive manpower services. Prime sponsors are cities and counties of 100, 000 or more, and consortia, defined as any combination of government units in which one member has a population of 100, 000 or more. A state may be a prime sponsor for areas not covered by local governments.

The prime sponsor must submit a comprehensive plan acceptable to the Secretary of Labor. The plan must set forth the kinds of programs and services to be offered and give assurances that manpower services will be provided to unemployed, underemployed, and disadvantaged persons most in need of help.

The sponsor must also set up a planning council representing local interests to serve in an advisory capacity.

The mix and design of services is to be determined by the sponsor, who may continue to fund programs of demonstrated effectiveness or set up new ones.

Eighty percent of the funds authorized under this Title are apportioned in accordance with a formula based on previous levels of funding, unemployment, and low income. The 20 percent not under the formula are to be distributed as follows: 5 percent for special grants for vocational education, 4 percent for state manpower services, and 5 percent to encourage consortia. The remaining amount is available at the Secretary's discretion.

State governments must establish a state manpower services council to review the plans of prime sponsors and make recommendations for coordination and for the cooperation of state agencies.

Title II provides funds to hire unemployed and underemployed persons in public service jobs in areas of substantial unemployment. Title III provides for direct federal supervision of manpower programs for Indians, migrant and seasonal farm workers, and special groups, such as youth, offenders, older workers, persons of limited English-speaking ability, and other disadvantaged. This title also gives the Secretary the responsibility for research, evaluation, experimental and demonstration projects, labor market information, and job-bank programs. Title IV continues the Job Corps. Title V establishes a National Manpower Commission. Title VI, added in December 1974 under the Emergency Jobs and Unemployment Assistance Act, authorizes a one-year appropriation of $2. 5 billion for a public service employment program for all areas, not just for areas of substantial unemployment. Title VII contains provisions applicable to all programs, such as prohibitions against discrimination and political activity.

embarked upon a drive for revenue-sharing legislation.
CETA was viewed as the first of several special revenue-
sharing programs. Third, state and local governments,
generally bypassed in manpower programs, were interested in assuming a strategic role. Finally the
Watergate crisis loosened rigidly held positions and
made differences between the legislative and executive
branches of governments easier to resolve.

Although opinions differ as to whether CETA is in
fact a revenue-sharing program, it is generally agreed
that its purpose is to shift control over the multibillion-
dollar manpower program, within broad limits, from
federal to local officials and to increase flexibility in
the use of these resources by local prime sponsors.

The rationale for the key elements of the legislation--
decentralization and decategorization--is both pragmatic
and ideological. The pragmatists assume that local
control is a superior way to plan and administer manpower programs. It was expected that programs would
be designed to meet local needs, that ineffective ones
would be weeded out, that comprehensive programs
would replace fragmented ones, and that innovations
would be introduced.

The ideological underpinning is the belief that a
decentralized system is a better expression of popular
will. It was assumed that under CETA there would be
greater community involvement and that local decision
makers would be more closely attuned to the electorate
and to the clients served.

EXTENT OF DECATEGORIZATION
AND DECENTRALIZATION

Although the purpose of the new legislation is to
provide training and employment opportunities through
a decategorized and decentralized system, CETA in fact
still operates to a large extent through categorical programs and with substantial federal involvement. Of the
four titles in the original statute that authorize operating
programs, three establish programs for special purposes or for particular groups. Title II sets up a public

employment program for areas of substantial unemployment; Title III authorizes programs for Indians, migratory farm workers, and other groups with special
problems; Title IV continues the Job Corps for disadvantaged youths. However, the Act permits prime
sponsors to interchange funds among several Titles. [2]

Title I (Comprehensive Manpower Services), which
is the main focus of this report, authorizes a decategorized manpower system. It replaces numerous programs, each with its own set of regulations and supportive bureaucracy, with a flexible system of
manpower services. However, the extent of decategorization that actually occurs locally rests with the
prime sponsors. They are free to retain or establish
as few or as many special programs as they deem
necessary.

In terms of funding, 34 percent of the original
fiscal 1975 CETA appropriation went to titles that authorize categorical programs. However, the enactment of
a special public service employment program (Title VI)
in December 1974[3] and appropriations for a summer
youth program radically altered the picture. Now 58
percent of CETA funds are earmarked for special use.
Thus, before CETA was well off the ground, it was
turned back toward a prescribed system of specific
programs for special problems.

Congressional intent to shift control of programs
and funds from federal to state and local authorities was
originally reflected only in Titles I and II. The addition
of Title VI and a summer youth program as decentralized (although categorized) activities brought the proportion of CETA resources managed by local authorities to
89 percent in fiscal 1975. [4]

[2] The act permits use of Title II and Title VI (Public Service Employment) funds for Title I (Comprehensive
Manpower Services) or Title IIIA (Special Target Groups)
programs at the option of the prime sponsor, while Title I
funds may be used for public service employment.

[3] Emergency Jobs and Unemployment Assistance Act of
1974.

[4] Some funds authorized by those titles are for the discretionary distribution by the Secretary of Labor (see Table
3, p. 33).

Although Congress clearly intended to decentralize most manpower programs, the nature and degree of this local autonomy is qualified. It was not expected that the Department of Labor would simply "put the money on the stump and run." On the contrary, the act explicitly provides for federal oversight responsibilities and has built specific intervention points, such as the approval of local plans, into the administrative process. In addition, there are detailed regulations and other requirements that set limits on the degree of local freedom.

The line between local control and federal oversight responsibilities is not finely drawn and this irresolution is reflected in the relationship between prime sponsors on the one hand, and local program operators and regional offices of the Manpower Administration on the other. Complete prime sponsor control would require that the independence of individual local project operators be subordinated to prime sponsor authority, and that regional office control be replaced by an oversight and technical assistance role. The survey findings suggest that the first condition has been met, the second only partially so.

There seemed to be a general uncertainty on the part of federal as well as local officials as to the appropriate role of regional offices. The survey found considerable variation, ranging from domination to neutrality, in the extent to which regional staff were involved in local programs. Differences are explained by the unequal capabilities of prime sponsors as well as varying perceptions of role by federal staff. The pressure of time, the urgency of meeting planning schedules, changes in national program directions, and new legislation brought with them bursts of federal activity.

Some prime sponsors believe the amount of regulation, the number of reports, and the federal presence in general to be excessive; a few felt that these might reverse the decentralization of manpower programs. What some viewed as undue interposition, others considered a reasonable exercise of oversight responsibilities. The gray area between these views may become reconciled and the relationship between the principals

more comfortable as prime sponsors gain experience
and regional offices adjust to a more modest role.

On balance, the early CETA program appears to
be neither completely decategorized nor completely decentralized, yet significant strides have been taken,
especially in decentralization. Institutions are being
built that will set new forces into motion and generate
additional changes.

CETA PLANNING: EXPECTATIONS AND FINDINGS

Inherent in the rationale for a decentralized system
is the premise that local authorities are in the best position to understand needs for manpower services, and
to plan and provide them.

In a situation of local control, planning was presumed
to be more relevant to community needs, more closely
related to decision making, and more integrated into
local government activities. What has happened under
Title I becomes clearer if a distinction is made between
the preparation of a specific planning document and planning as a continuing process.

There is little evidence to indicate that the first
formal CETA plans were markedly superior to their
predecessors, in some cases they were strikingly similar. Given the constraints in terms of time, staff, and
know-how with which the CETA planner had to cope, a
different outcome is difficult to envision. In the few
weeks (somtimes days) that the prime sponsors' staffs
were given to prepare the grant applications, there was
hardly time to do more than dig out, adapt, and staple
together existing material. Moreover, most prime
sponsors were unable to start with a clean slate; there
were ongoing programs to consider. Under the unremit-
ting pressure to meet deadlines, many CETA planners
did little more than provide, pro forma, the items necessary to pass muster and trigger the allocation of funds.
Second-year operations may provide a better basis for
assessing manpower plans in a decentralized system.

When manpower planning is viewed as a process,
CETA planning represents the latest stage in a

development that started with the Cooperative Area Manpower Planning System (CAMPS) in the mid-1960s. Pre-CETA planning, even at its most advanced, was primarily an information exchange far removed from the locus of power and with very little effect on decision making. The planning system under CETA, however, is closely integrated into the local government structure and planners have access to the prime sponsors. In many cases CETA planners are also manpower administrators and decision makers.

Decentralization is welcomed not only by practical administrators who see it as a more effective way of conducting manpower business, but also by those who equate decentralization with a more democratic system. It was assumed that decision making would be brought closer to the people by publishing CETA plans, providing an opportunity to comment on them, establishing advisory councils, and placing program control in the hands of elected officials answerable to the community. Decentralization implies that the smaller the unit of government, the closer it can be to the people and thus the more representative of their interests.

On the whole, the publication of CETA plans in newspapers was a formality and the exposure of the plans for comments, largely cosmetic. Time pressure precluded the possibility of any meaningful participation from the public. Faced with a choice between full ventilation of plans and speedy implementation of the program, the prime sponsors opted for the latter, perhaps on the assumption that the additional time required for comments would not produce significantly greater public involvement.

Public advisory councils, which Congress hoped would become the instrument for community participation in all aspects of CETA, were established. Although the scope of their responsibilities is wider than their pre-CETA counterparts, the membership is much the same and their role remains advisory. The survey found that, in the main, they tend to be passive. The dominant influence on the councils is usually exercised by the CETA administrator and staff. Nevertheless, CETA councils are more viable than their predecessors; their role and composition are legitimized by legislation; they are

concerned with a wide range of activities and are closer
to the decision makers; in a few places they have exercised considerable independent influence.

ADMINISTERING LOCAL PROGRAMS

For decentralization of whatever degree to become
operational, prime sponsors must establish the necessary administrative machinery to assume command of
the manpower programs in their jurisdictions--this has
largely been accomplished. Units have been set up in
all areas to handle centrally such administrative functions as fiscal accounting, reporting, and contract
supervision.

Many prime sponsors have gone further and consolidated or coordinated recruitment, referral, job development, and placement services. In a few cases, the
prime sponsors have designed a comprehensive manpower program. Decentralization of federal programs
seems to be accompanied by centralization at the local
level.

How well prime sponsor control is being exercised
and what the effect of decentralization is on program
operations have yet to be established. It is clear that
the new responsibilities are seriously straining the capabilities of the local governments, half of whom had no
prior experience with what are now Title I programs. An
assessment of 402 prime sponsors made by the Department of Labor Manpower Administration in May 1975
found 114 to be marginal performers; 52 were characterized as "significant underperformers." (A later survey, made in September, showed that most of these had
brought their programs up to acceptable levels. The
number of marginal performers had dropped to 19, and
only 3 remained on the list of significant underperformers.)

Survey responses cited as major obstacles inexperience, the complexity of the programs, cumbersome and
changing procedures, and repeated program interruptions occasioned by funding changes and new legislation.
The enactment of Title VI and the all-out push for public service employment programs overwhelmed many
prime sponsors in their efforts to implement Title I.

In vesting control in state and local prime sponsors, Congress stipulated that organizations operating manpower programs before CETA would not necessarily continue to manage them.   There were to be no "presumptive deliverers" of manpower services.   This position, it was assumed, would result in competition for program contracts and selection by the prime sponsor of the best performers; however, there was some equivocating on this point. Although prime sponsors are given authority to contract with organizations best able to deliver services, the statute urges maximum feasible use of existing agencies. Some Manpower Administration regional offices have delayed approval of prime sponsor plans on this issue.

The study results indicate that although, on the whole, the same program operators were used, important changes did occur.   Most significant is the role of prime sponsors.   In addition to centralizing administrative functions, many began to conduct their own programs. This occurred mainly at the expense of local employment service offices and community action agencies.

On the other hand, community-based organizations such as the Urban League, Opportunities Industrialization Center, and Services, Employment, and Redevelopment benefited from more funds and an increase in the number of local programs.   Along with other program operators, however, they lost some degree of freedom they enjoyed as independent sponsors funded directly by the federal government.   CETA has added an administrative layer between program operators and the Department of Labor.   Some community-based organizations are uneasy about the trend towards consolidation, which they see as a threat to their identity as agencies serving special racial and ethnic groups.

According to the Department of Labor estimates, 1,970 organizations were directly funded by local prime sponsors in fiscal 1975 to provide manpower services under Title I--500 more service deliverers than were operating prior to CETA.   The net increase results from 720 new service deliverers and a decrease of 210 that were not selected.   This proliferation reflects the funding of programs for the first time, especially in counties, and the decisions of many prime sponsors to deliver

some services to participants through their own staff
units.
    The shift of control from federal to local levels was
expected to lead to greater involvement of elected officials in manpower matters. There has undoubtedly been
increased participation, but in most cases it has been
limited to key decisions such as hiring a CETA administrator and allocation of local manpower resources among
programs and client groups.
    CETA decentralized political as well as program
responsibility. Placing the manpower program under
the aegis of state and local elected officials puts it in
the political arena and subjects it to the local political
process. Local elected officials tend to be more accessible than federal administrators and perhaps more susceptible to politically potent groups with interests to
protect or to advance. However, the political process
is subject to abuse at any level, and the survey did find
some instances of political patronage, but this was not
typical of Title I programs.

CETA PARTICIPANTS

    It is too early to tell whether local control will
result in better job preparation for the labor market--
the most important question in assessing manpower programs. It is possible, however, to detect some changes
in the kinds of people being served under Title I. The
manpower program clients before CETA were nearly all
poor, with little job experience or training. Participants
in Title I are higher on the socioeconomic ladder; relatively fewer of the disadvantaged, youth, and high school
dropouts are being enrolled. These findings are consistent with the direction of forces impinging upon CETA,
such as: 1) broader eligibility requirements, 2) greater
participation of suburban communities, 3) increasing use
of programs by victims of the recession, and 4) the inclination of some program managers to enroll persons
most likely to succeed rather than those most in need of
manpower training. There are some countervailing
pressures, such as the influence of community-based

organizations, the personal commitment of some CETA
staff to serve minorities and the disadvantaged, and the
intervention of some regional offices.

EFFECTS OF DECATEGORIZATION

Decategorization and decentralization are comple-
mentary. To decentralize without giving localities the
freedom to put together a mix of programs tailored to
local needs would be to provide the trappings but not the
substance of local control. CETA furnishes this flexibility by decategorizing earlier specialized programs.

Besides enabling the prime sponsor to fashion programs relevant to local needs, decategorization was expected to: 1) eliminate the duplication characteristic of
earlier programs; 2) encourage new programs that are
comprehensive, organizationally integrated, and liberally
laced with innovations; and 3) eliminate or modify inadequate programs.

Despite their newly acquired authority and flexibility,
prime sponsors did not rush to reshape manpower programs. Their flexibility was circumscribed by internal
and external constraints. Insufficient time, lack of staff
and experience, institutional pressures, and political
considerations all operated against change. Most important, prime sponsors inherited a full complement of
programs that could not immediately be turned around.
Most programs were therefore continued, although some
were stripped of their intake, administrative, and job
placement functions; they were often consolidated and
centralized. Because certain groups of clients require
specialized manpower services, some categorical programs may well be indicated. The objections to pre-
CETA programs referred to overlapping activities and
lack of integration rather than to special programs as
such.

Notwithstanding the pressures facing sponsors, they
have been able to adjust quickly to a changing labor market. This has been demonstrated by their ability to
shift from on-the-job training to work experience projects
as the recession developed and deepened.

EMERGING ISSUES

Changing Nature of Program and Clientele

A number of issues have begun to emerge in the early transition period. Perhaps most important is the shifting of manpower programs away from the chronic, structural problems of the labor market toward an increasing emphasis on the immediate cyclical problem of unemployment. This change was accompanied by a broadening of eligibility for manpower services.

Social, economic, and political developments all played a part in this new orientation. The social ferment of the 1960s and the organizational support for social action had diminished to a considerable extent. Governmental enthusiasm for "Great Society" programs dampened and public interest in coping with the problems of the disadvantaged waned, particularly since instant cures did not materialize.

Soon after the enactment of CETA, the economy faltered badly. Employment opportunities for graduates of manpower programs declined. It was difficult to persuade employers to accept on-the-job trainees while they were laying off their regular work force. The ranks of manpower program applicants swelled with newly unemployed workers who did not normally compete for slots in those programs. The response of prime sponsors to these conditions was to concentrate on subsidized work experience and public service employment programs.

On the political level, the looser eligibility requirements of CETA and the delegation of decision making to some 400 elected officials invited a broader participation in manpower programs. The addition of a large public service employment program (Title VI) changed the emphasis of manpower programs from its earlier structural to a counter-cyclical orientation. The shift was welcomed by local officials who recognized the political attractiveness of a program that not only created jobs but also could be used to provide fiscal relief for hard-pressed communities.

The change in the nature of manpower programs and participants suggests a retreat from the 10-year effort to grapple with the employability problems of the disadvantaged. It raises the question of how to insulate the hard-core unemployed from the competition of better prepared program applicants.

A closely related issue is the advisability of addressing the problems of cyclical unemployment (Title VI) through a program (CETA) designed principally to deal with labor market maladjustments of a structural nature. Incorporating a public service employment component into CETA is consistent with the general objective of designing a comprehensive manpower system, and increases the prime sponsor's options in dealing with local manpower matters. Presumably, efficiency of program administration would also be increased. On the other hand, Title VI is basically a different kind of program for a different group, authorized for a more limited time period. The relative attractiveness of its job-creation program puts other less glamorous programs at a disadvantage in terms of the time, interest, and attention of the prime sponsors. Finally, housing both programs together tends to obscure the differences between structural and cyclical manpower programs.

Tendencies to bifurcate the system of manpower programs are already discernible. There are distinctions between the work-ready applicants enrolled in public service employment programs and those less prepared who are placed in pre-employment training activities. Moreover, the two kinds of programs are frequently administered through separate organizational units.

Issues in Public Service Employment

Although most of the field work for this study was completed before the enactment of Title VI, there was some opportunity to identify a number of issues associated with public service employment. The most serious obstacle to the attainment of the Title VI objective of creating additional jobs is likely to be the practice of substitution; that is, there are increasing indications that federal funds are being used for positions that might otherwise have been financed through regular local revenues--not to create new jobs. However, some local jurisdictions are experiencing actual budget stringencies and unavoidable layoffs.

There are also worrisome institutional problems. Conflicts between the objectives of a national public service employment program and the interests of established institutions in the public sector are not uncommon. Most of these arise from the relationship between CETA enrollees and the regular civil service employees with respect to civil service hiring qualifications, entry-level jobs, promotional opportunities, and the order of layoffs.

Political patronage, if not the most serious problem to emerge, is probably the most publicized one. Some indications appeared early in the Title I program. However, opportunities for such practices are much greater in the public service employment program and will be covered in the next phase of the study.

National Policies and Local Decisions

Framers of the original CETA legislation faced the problem of reconciling a commitment to local discretion with the need to address national problems. In the absence of any new major development, it was assumed that programs fashioned by 400 prime sponsors would be congruent with national needs and priorities.

However, Congressional action since CETA suggests an inclination to revert to a categorical approach in meeting new national developments. The enactment of the public service employment program as a new categorical title is one indication of this tendency; handling the summer youth program through a separate appropriation is another.

The problems associated with public service programs (especially that of substitution) and the proclivity to spin off new and visible programs have generated new initiatives in Congressional committees. The chairman of the House subcommittee dealing with manpower has drafted legislation to extend and enlarge the public service employment program, as well as to centralize control in the regional offices of the Department of Labor. Funding would be made to a wider spectrum of public bodies as

well as to private nonprofit organizations. In effect, a
large part of the manpower program would be recentral-
ized. The ranking minority member of the subcommittee
has introduced legislation that would establish a series of
national categorical programs. Taken together, they
could spell recentralization and recategorization. Although these are not yet fixed positions, they do suggest
the way the Congressional wind is blowing.

Other Issues

In addition to the general issues just discussed, a
number of specific problems are coming into focus.

The allocation of Title I resources is a potential
source of difficulty. Prime sponsors are guaranteed at
least 90 percent of their prior year's funding level. Despite this stabilizer, which tends to prevent abrupt
changes, at constant funding levels the amount available
for many large cities is likely to decrease over a period
of years. There are also technical problems in measuring unemployment and low income and in designing measures to allocate resources to those most in need.

Advisory councils are still struggling with identity
problems. Increasingly, the objectivity of council members whose agencies provide program services to the
prime sponsor is being questioned. In some instances
they have been excluded from council membership or
have not been permitted to vote on issues on which they
are an interested party.

The relationship between the employment service,
which had been the major pre-CETA manpower agency,
and the present prime sponsors is frequently unsettled,
especially in situations in which the role of the employment service has been eliminated or curtailed. Since
both have legislative authority--the employment service
under the Wagner Peyser Act and the prime sponsors
under CETA--duplication or stratification of services
may emerge. There are indications that some employment service agencies will focus on job-ready applicants,
leaving the less qualified for the prime sponsors. Such
possibilities invite the attention of the Congressional
committees whose jurisdictions encompass both programs.

Authority is not easily relinquished. This is particularly true of CETA, in which the transfer of control has not been accompanied by a clear distinction between the prerogatives of the prime sponsor and the responsibilities of the federal establishment. Both have been operating uneasily in the area between the reach of one and the grasp of the other. This testing of the limits of hegemony is likely to continue for some time.

SUMMARY

The impact of CETA on manpower programs is visible in changes in both structure and program.

Changes in Structure

- The overriding objective of CETA is decentralization and in large measure this has been accomplished. Despite serious administrative problems, state and local officials are assuming control of manpower programs. However, this authority is constrained by considerable federal presence. The performance of prime sponsors in terms of meeting their plans and discharging their administrative responsibilities leaves much to be desired. Over 40 percent had initially been assessed by the Department of Labor as being either marginal or unsatisfactory performers.
- Manpower is becoming institutionalized as a regular component of local governments.
- CETA has scrambled existing interorganizational relationships at all levels. Locally, the key manpower role has shifted to local elected officials at the expense of the Manpower Administration regional offices on one hand and local project operators on the other. Prime sponsors have been catapulted into substantive areas that had been the exclusive province of such agencies as the employment service and vocational education.
- Prime sponsors have centralized administrative functions under their immediate control and have

made significant progress in consolidating such
manpower services as client intake and job placement. Moreover, there is a growing tendency on
the part of prime sponsors to conduct programs.
- Manpower programs now under the aegis of local
elected officials are being drawn into the local
political process.

Changes in Program

- Resources available for the first year of CETA
were substantially greater than the level for manpower programs in fiscal 1974. Most of the increase is attributable to the new public service
employment program. However, Title I funding
is also 12 percent higher than the amount for comparable programs in 1974. In terms of relative
shares, Title I funds shifted during the first year
from the South to the West and Northeast and
from cities to counties. In general, counties are
assuming a much larger role in manpower affairs.
- The manpower planning process is better integrated with the local administrative and power
structure but the formal planning documents are
generally not well developed. By repeated modifications, plans are adjusted to mirror experience.
Consequently, the planning process tends to follow
rather than lead program development.
- Although CETA replaced the earlier mandated
categorical programs to encourage greater flexibility, local prime sponsors are continuing such
programs largely unchanged.
- CETA has broadened considerably the scope of
manpower activities in terms of places, programs,
and people. Geographically, the program has become universal; local flexibility and the addition
of a public service employment component has
widened the range of manpower programs. With
the loosening of eligibility requirements and the
impact of the recession, participation in manpower
programs has become more general.

- The character of manpower programs is changing
  from one preoccupied with the intractable employability problems of the disadvantaged to one increasingly concerned with the immediate cyclical
  problems of the unemployed generally. This
  shift is clearly discernible in Title II and Title VI.
  To a lesser but still perceptible degree, it is also
  true of Title I programs.

2
Resources and Allocations

Since the passage of the Manpower Development and Training Act of 1962 (MDTA) there has been a 60-fold increase in Department of Labor manpower program funding to $3.7 billion, reflecting changes in policy, the addition of specific programs, and responses to cyclical unemployment. While still only scratching the surface of the need, manpower programs now constitute a sizable component of the federal budget. How these funds are distributed and who is to exercise control have become very important questions. Chapter 2 reviews the resources available for manpower programs under the Comprehensive Employment and Training Act (CETA) in relation to similar programs in the past. Formulas for allocation prescribed in the act and some of the attendant issues are considered. The major focus is on the effects of the Title I formula on the nature and direction of manpower programs in fiscal 1975.

APPROPRIATIONS FOR MANPOWER PROGRAMS

Prior to fiscal 1975 funds for work and training programs administered by the Department of Labor were authorized by four statutes: the MDTA, the Economic Opportunity Act (EOA), the Emergency Employment Act

of 1971 (EEA), and the Social Security Act (for the Work
Incentive Program). Table 1 compares the total resources available for manpower programs before and
after CETA. The growing importance of public service
employment beginning in fiscal 1972 reflects recognition that new strategies were necessary to cope with
rising unemployment.

Table 1. Department of Labor Obligations for Work and
Training Programs, Fiscal Years 1963, 1970-1975 (amounts
in million dollars)

Fiscal Year	All Programs	Programs Corresponding with CETA				
		Total	Work and Training Programs	Public Employ-ment	Job Corps	WIN and Other
1963	56	56	56	-	-	-
1970	1,419	1,340	1,170	-	170	79
1971	1,485	1,421	1,261	-	160	64
1972	2,697	2,522	1,358	962	202	175
1973	2,754	2,545	1,113	1,239	193	209
1974 b/	2,144	1,884	1,453	281	150	260 a/
1975 b/	3,731	3,580	2,155	1,217	208	151 a/

Source: Manpower Report of the President, Table F-1,
        Manpower Administration, U. S. Dept. of Labor
a/ Includes funds for National Older Workers Program.
b/ Preliminary.

Despite its billing as a comprehensive manpower
program, CETA accounts for only 56 percent of all
federal manpower program funds. In fiscal 1975, according to Office of Management and Budget estimates, $6.8
billion was to be obligated by federal agencies for programs that fall broadly into the category of manpower,
including vocational rehabilitation, certain veterans'
benefits, and the employment service, as shown below:

Estimated Fiscal Year 1975 Obligations	Million Dollars	Percent
Federal Manpower Programs	$6,827	100
Department of Labor	4,590	67
Comprehensive Employment and Training Act	3,800	56

Source: Office of Management and Budget

Table 2 compares appropriations for CETA for fiscal 1975 with initial requests by the Administration and with appropriations for comparable activities in fiscal 1974. The total appropriation for fiscal 1975 was $3.7 billion-- $1.4 billion above the previous year. Increases were mainly for the temporary public service employment program (Title VI) and for the summer youth program.

The initial emphasis of CETA was to have been on Title I--comprehensive manpower programs. The Administration's request of $1.3 billion, including funds for summer youth programs, was less than the prior year's appropriation of $1.4 billion; Congress, however, raised the amount to close to $1.6 billion, a 12 percent increase over 1974. Later $473 million was added for summer programs. Thus the total of Title I plus summer youth programs came to about $2.1 billion--46 percent more than for corresponding programs in fiscal 1974.

The public service employment component of CETA (Title II) consisted originally of a modest program confined to areas of substantial unemployment. However, as unemployment shot up, Congress passed the Emergency Jobs and Unemployment Assistance Act of 1974 (EJUAA), which authorized $2.5 billion for public service jobs for unemployed persons in all areas,[5] and extended the expiring Emergency Employment Act for a year.

Chart 1 shows the extent of decategorization and decentralization possible under CETA: 42 percent of

[5] $1 billion was appropriated for fiscal 1975; of this amount $125 million was to be transferred to the Department of Commerce for public works projects.

Table 2.   Fiscal Year 1974 and Fiscal Year 1975 Appropriations for Comparable Manpower Programs (amounts
in million dollars)

Activity	Fiscal Year 1974 Appro- priation	Fiscal Year 1975		Change From Fiscal Year 1974
		Initial Request	Appro- priation	
Comprehensive Manpower Assis- tance (Title I)	1, 407	1, 319	1, 580	+ 173
Public Service Em- ployment Emergency Em- ployment Act (PEP)	250	-	-	- 250
Substantial Unem- ployment Areas (Title II)	370	350	400	+ 30
Emergency Jobs (Title VI)	-	1, 000	875	+ 875
National Programs (Title III)	213 (397)a/	210	243b/	+ 30
Summer Youth		-	473b/	+ 473
Job Corps (Title IV)	150	171	171	+ 21
TOTAL	2, 390	3, 050	3, 742	+1, 352

Source: Manpower Administration, U. S. Dept. of Labor
a/ Included in the $1, 407 million figure for comprehen-
    sive manpower assistance.
b/ Includes $17 million to be transferred to the Com-
    munity Services Administration.

CHART 1. Amounts Authorized for Program
Activities Under the Comprehensive Employment
and Training Act, Fiscal Year 1975

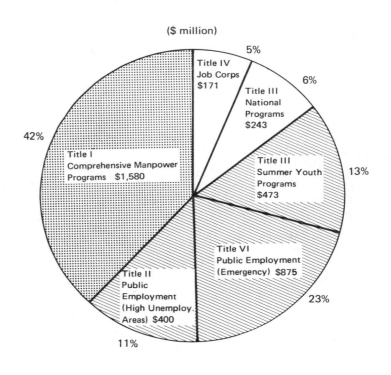

($ million)

Title IV
Job Corps
$171

5%

Title III
National
Programs
$243

6%

Title I
Comprehensive Manpower
Programs $1,580

42%

Title III
Summer Youth
Programs
$473

13%

Title VI
Public Employment
(Emergency) $875

23%

Title II
Public
Employment
(High Unemploy.
Areas) $400

11%

DECATEGORIZED 42%

DECENTRALIZED 89%

the funds are available without program restrictions; 58 percent of the money is earmarked for specific program categories, such as public service jobs, summer youth programs, the Job Corps, and national programs. Eighty-nine percent of the funds (Titles I, II, VI, and summer youth) are under state and local control, and 11 percent of the money is managed by the federal government. However, the 89 percent which is theoretically decentralized is administered with a considerable degree of federal regulation and oversight, as discussed in subsequent chapters.

There is no unanimity as to how much local autonomy and flexibility is desirable. However, recent Congressional action, including additional funds for the Emergency Employment Act (EEA), the passage of Title VI, and authorization for summer programs suggests a tendency on the part of Congress to respond to emerging problems with categorical programs. There is apparently a feeling that locally perceived needs may not coincide with national priorities.

TITLE I ALLOCATION FORMULA

The impact of manpower resources is measured not only by the total amount available but also by the manner in which it is distributed. Basically there are two ways in in which resources have been allocated: by formula and at the discretion of the Secretary of Labor.

Under CETA, funds for Titles I, II, and VI (the decentralized programs) are allocated among prime sponsors by formula, although the prescription is different for each title and some funds are reserved for discretionary use. Funds for Titles III and IV (the centralized programs) are not disbursed at the discretion of the Department of Labor.

Before CETA, MDTA classroom training funds were allotted by formula to the states, which were then responsible for a "pass through" to local sponsors, generally the employment service offices and the schools. EEA appropriations were also assigned in a prescribed

fashion to states and eligible local government units. 6/
On the other hand, EOA funds were not subject to formula
allocation.

There are nonmonetary as well as monetary consequences of a distribution of resources based upon a
formula. Such distribution universalizes the manpower
program; localities not previously involved in any significant way are now encompassed. A formula also mini-
mizes the effect of political and vested interest clout as
well as grantsmanship, and permits the federal administrator to make decisions in a more objective manner.
However, if pressure at the federal level is reduced, the
reverse is true for the state and local prime sponsors
who now have full responsibility for distribution of resources within their jurisdictions. Local interest groups
can be expected to compete for limited resources.
Finally, formula allocation does not permit flexibility in
meeting special needs. Resources previously concentrated on limited programs and specific client groups
may be spread too thin for effective results.

Given the decision to use a formula, its nature and
effects become critically significant. The framers of
the CETA legislation debated the most appropriate Title
I allocation formula. The issues were which elements
to use--unemployment or low income--and how to maintain stability in the funding process while permitting
sufficient flexibility to adjust to rapidly changing economic conditions. 7/

The political imperative of securing sufficient votes
for passage also subjected the specifics of the CETA
formula to considerable horse trading. The formula had
to stand the test of geopolitics as well as the practical
tests of feasibility. The elements of the formula and the

6/ Cities and counties of 75,000 were eligible program
    agents under EEA. State governments were desig-
    nated as program agents for parts of states not cov-
    ered by other sponsors. EEA established the precedent
    for formula allocations to local units of government.
7/ See Robert Guttman, "Intergovernmental Relations
    Under the New Manpower Act," Monthly Labor Review
    97(6):10-16, 1974.

weights given to each significantly affect the key question
of who gets how much. The availability of uniform statistical data to measure need was also an important consideration in arriving at factors to be used.

The bill originally passed by the House contained
only two elements in the Title I formula: the prior year's
funding level and unemployment. The House Education
and Labor Committee believed that the level of unemployment was an adequate proxy for various forms of disadvantage in the labor market. The Senate bill, however,
proposed unemployment and poverty as the principal
criteria. The House bill worked in favor of those states
and regions where unemployment rather than low income
is relatively more prevalent. The Senate preferred to
maintain the poverty emphasis of manpower programs.

The Title I formula finally agreed upon was a compromise that gave precedence to past levels of funding over
measures of economic distress. Having agreed that 80
percent of the funds were to be allocated, the House and
Senate adopted the following Title I formula:[8/]

- 50 percent to be allocated according to the relative share of the prime sponsor's prior year's
  funds.
- 37. 5 percent to be allocated according to the
  relative share of U. S. unemployment.
- 12. 5 percent to be based on the relative number
  of adults in low-income families.

Thus half of the resources were used to avoid severe
program dislocation during the transition. This concern
with stability and program practicalities is reinforced by
the requirement that no prime sponsor may get more than
150 percent nor less than 90 percent of the previous year's

[8/] One percent of the 80 percent allocated by formula was
    to be reserved for state prime sponsors for support of
    state manpower services councils. Not less than $2
    million was to be allotted among Guam, the Virgin
    Islands, American Samoa, and the Trust Territories of
    the Pacific Islands.

funding._9/_ The Secretary of Labor is required to use
part of his discretionary funds to "hold harmless" prime
sponsor manpower programs at 90 percent of last year's
level.

However equitable or inequitable this distribution
may have been, it was considered politically and program-
matically essential to prevent abrupt losses of funds and
programs in some areas and extraordinary gains in others.
Legislators needed the stability to marshall support for
the bill, the Administration wanted it to facilitate implementation of programs, and project sponsors saw it as a
means to retain their programs.

Serious consequences of the 90 percent minimum
and the 150 percent maximum limitations soon became
apparent. If the total amount to be allocated remains
constant, the effect of the 90 percent minimum applied
successively for several years would be to lower the
amount each year until a point is reached at which adjustments are no longer needed. Similarly, those areas to
which the 150 percent maximum is applied would get more
each year until the adjustment would no longer be needed.

The Manpower Administration estimates that in four
or five years, assuming no change in available funds or
in relative unemployment and poverty, all areas would
have reached their ultimate share based on the factors in
the formula, and the adjustment process would end. The
point of equilibrium would vary for each area. Some
areas might drop to as low as 50 percent of manpower
funds in the 1974 base year, while others might end up
with more than double their original amount.

The effect would be that many areas would gradually
settle at a lower level than before CETA unless Title I
appropriations are increased every year. Other areas,
eligible for the 150 percent maximum, would continue to
increase in their level of funding. The differential effects of the formula and adjustments are discussed more
fully later in this chapter.

_9/_ An exception to the maximum is allowed if 150 per-
       cent of the prior year's funding level is less than 50
       percent of the amount that the prime sponsor would
       be entitled to under the formula.

Although 20 percent of Title I funds are not subject to allocation by formula, the discretionary use of this money by the Secretary of Labor is tightly circumscribed. The statute requires that these funds be used for consortium incentives (5 percent), supplemental vocational education (5 percent), and state manpower services (4 perpercent). 10/ The remainder is available for discretionary use, including the 90 percent hold-harmless adjustment.

MEASUREMENT OF UNEMPLOYMENT AND POVERTY

One of the reasons for selecting the number of unemployed and the number of adults in low-income families as elements in the Title I formula was the assurance by the Administration that it was possible to obtain current statistics on a political subdivision level. Nevertheless there are serious technical problems with both factors that affect their usefulness as measures of economic need.

Next to the 50 percent weight given to the past year's funding level, the Title I formula places the greatest reliance on unemployment statistics. This decision has been questioned by those who maintain that the standard concepts and methods used do not adequately measure the full extent of unemployment. The unemployment figures do not include discouraged workers who have ceased looking for work because they believe no work is available. Persons on part-time work schedules who want full-time work and persons who earn too little to provide a "minimum adequate" level of living--those who might be considered underemployed rather than unemployed--are also left out of the unemployment calculation. Presumably the third element of the formula--adults in low-income families--is designed to reflect the discouraged workers and the underemployed, but this element has a weight of only 12.5 percent in the formula.

Since the level of unemployment significantly affects the distribution of CETA funds, prime sponsors have

10/ See p. 3 for a definition of consortium.

become very conscious of the method by which unemployment is measured. Two methods of estimating jobless-
ness have been available from the Department of Labor:
a derived method used in the Manpower Administration
and a survey method used by the Bureau of Labor
Statistics (BLS).

The derived method is one used by state employment
service analysts to estimate unemployment for local
labor market areas. Essentially, it is a building-block
method which starts with the number of insured unemployed and estimates those not covered under unemployment insurance. The survey method is used to arrive
at an estimate of unemployment for the U. S. based on
the Census Bureau's monthly Current Population Survey
(CPS) of a national sample of households.

In 1973, responsibility for the method of estimating
local as well as national labor force and unemployment
was assigned to BLS in order to reconcile the two series.
The major change introduced by BLS in measuring unemployment was the use of benchmark figures obtained from
the Current Population Survey for the largest states,
metropolitan areas, and counties. The Bureau also
changed the basis of estimating employment from "place
of work" to "place of residence." Estimates of the number of unemployed and the rate of unemployment obtained
by the BLS revisions differ from those arrived at by the
method formerly used by the Manpower Administration. 11/
Indeed, the Department of Labor is being challenged in
court by the state of New Jersey, which claims that the
revised method tends to lower its unemployment estimates and therefore its proportionate share of CETA funds.

The second element of need in the Title I formula
(adults in low-income families) also has measurement

11/ James R. Wetzel and Martin Ziegler, "Measuring
     Unemployment in States and Local Areas," Monthly
     Labor Review 97(6):40-46, 1974. See also "Report
     to the Senate Committee on Labor and Public Wel-
     fare and to the House Committee on Education and
     Labor, as Specified in CETA, Section 312(f)." Ap-
     pendix B of Manpower Report of the President, 1975
     (Washington, D. C.: U. S. Department of Labor,
     1975), pp. 183-189.

problems. Low income is defined in the act as family income of $7,000 in 1969, updated for subsequent years by changes in the Consumer Price Index. The $7,000 figure was selected as being close to the Bureau of Labor Statistics' estimate of the annual cost for the lower budget for a four-person urban family in 1969.

Congress selected the $7,000 figure as the low-income criterion instead of the more familiar poverty-level threshold. The choice of this criterion and the relatively low weight (12.5 percent) assigned to the low-income factor influenced the distribution of Title I funds. For example, the South had 40 percent of the adults in "low-income" families, but 44 percent of the adults in "poverty" families. Had Congress decided to use the poverty instead of the low-income criterion, the South's share would have been higher. The use of a higher weight for the low-income factor in the Title I formula would also have given low-income regions a larger share of manpower funds. 12/

For fiscal 1976, it was necessary to update these figures to 1973, using a low-income cutoff of $8,000 based on the rise in the Consumer Price Index, and a revised estimate of families with incomes below this figure based on the Census Bureau's annual survey of household incomes.

There are several problems in estimating the number of adults in low-income families: 1) the use of a uniform standard for low-income families that does not take into account farm/nonfarm differences in living expenditures; 2) the lack of local detail in the Current Population Survey, which is used as a change factor; estimates for local areas must be calculated from state or regional figures; 3) the time lag of approximately two years (1973 income figures being used for 1976 allocations); and 4) technical problems in arriving at family budget estimates.

CETA itself recognizes the technical deficiencies in the estimates of unemployment and low income. It requires the Department of Labor to develop 1) reliable

12/ See also The Job Ahead, Manpower Policies in the South (Southern Regional Council, 1975).

methods to measure unemployment, underemployment, and labor demand for states, local areas, and poverty areas; 2) data to construct an annual statistical measure of labor market related economic hardship; and 3) methods to maintain more comprehensive household budget data, including a level of adequacy, to reflect regional and rural/urban differences in household living. [13]/

TITLE II AND TITLE VI ALLOCATION FORMULAS

Since Title II (public service employment) is limited to areas of substantial unemployment, Congressional deliberations centered mainly on the identification of such areas rather than the formula to be used for allocation of funds. The definition agreed upon was similar to that used in Section 6 of the EEA: any area experiencing an unemployment rate of 6.5 percent or more for three consecutive months. [14]/

The single element of the Title II formula is the relative number of unemployed in each substantial unemployment area. While this formula is not so controversial as that of Title I, there are three problems. One is the question of whether sufficient weight is given to degrees of unemployment above 6.5 percent. This is particularly germane in a period of high unemployment, when national unemployment rates exceed 8 percent. The act permits the 20 percent discretionary fund to be used for this purpose, but its application is not automatic.

Seasonality presents a second problem. The use of a three-month period for calculating unemployment and designating Title II areas is anomalous since the purpose is to aid areas with chronic unemployment, not those areas with temporary seasonal fluctuations. The third problem is the difficulty of identifying pockets of high unemployment in a standard way.

13/ Section 312.
14/ Under EEA, Section 6 funds were allotted to areas with unemployment rates of 6 percent or more for three consecutive months.

Title VI, authorized by the Emergency Jobs and Unemployment Assistance Act, was designed to respond quickly to cyclical unemployment--to make the greatest impact on creating public service jobs for an emergency period. Unemployment is the only criterion. The formula has three parts: 50 percent to be allotted to prime sponsors based on the total volume of unemployment; 25 percent based on unemployment in excess of 4.5 percent of the labor force in each area; and 25 percent to substantial unemployment areas eligible under Title II. The weights are a compromise between the House and Senate versions of the bill (see Table 3). The Title VI formula, unlike that of Title II, gives a boost to areas with most severe unemployment. Only 10 percent of Title VI funds are reserved for discretionary use in meeting new unemployment crises.

In summary, there are a number of issues in the CETA allocation formulas: technical problems in estimating unemployment and numbers of adults in low-income

Table 3. Elements and Weights in CETA Allocation Formulas, Titles I, II, and VI

Discretionary and Formula Amounts	Percent Distribution		
	Title I	Title II	Title VI
Discretionary amount	20	20	10
Formula amount	80	80	90
Total	100	100	100
Formula elements:			
Prior year's funds	50	-	-
Adults in low-income	$12\frac{1}{2}$	-	-
Number unemployed	$37\frac{1}{2}$	-	50
Above 4.5% rate	-	-	25
Areas of subst. unempl. a/	-	100	25
Total	100	100	100

a/ Areas with unemployment rate of 6.5 percent or more for 3 consecutive months.

families; seasonality in the Title II formula; lack of a
"severity" factor under Title II; and the erosion of funds
for some areas despite the 90 percent hold-harmless
feature of Title I.   Perhaps the most important question
is the distributive effect, which is discussed in the following section.

EFFECT OF TITLE I FORMULA

States and Regions

Although the Title I formula has stabilizers that tend
to maintain consistency from year to year, its use has
resulted in shifts in resources that are having an effect
on the places and people who receive manpower services.
Of the $1.6 billion appropriated for Title I in fiscal 1975,
$1.2 billion was distributed by formula to prime sponsors.
Discretionary funds were added for the 90 percent hold-
harmless adjustments, making the total $1.4 billion.
Thus total resources available under Title I of CETA
were higher than the 1974 base, but the amount distributed
by formula was lower (see Table 4).

Because of the heavy weight (50 percent) given to the
prior year's allotment of manpower funds, the rank order
of states, in terms of the percentage of total funds received, is with few exceptions the same as that in fiscal
1974 even before the 90 percent hold-harmless adjustment
was made. 15/   Table 5 suggests, however, that there was
a slight tilt in favor of states receiving most of the 1974
funds (first quintile) for programs comparable to Title I
of CETA.

Table 6 shows, nevertheless, that some geographic
shifts are taking place in the regional pattern. Most significant are declines in the relative share of the southern
regions, and relative gains in the west coast and northeast regions.

The effect of the 90 percent minimum--150 percent
maximum adjustments on individual areas is to mitigate
changes due to the formula. After adjustment, all states

15/ Spearman's rank correlation ρ = .99

Table 4. CETA Title I Funds Available and Allocated,
Fiscal Year 1975 (amounts in million dollars)

Appropriation and Allocation Title I	Fiscal Year 1975	Percent of Fiscal Year 1974 Manpower Funds[a]
Appropriation	1, 580	112
Formula allocation		
Formula amount	1, 249	89
Adjusted amount[b]	1, 354	96
Non-formula allocations		
State vocational education	79	-
State manpower services	63	-
Consortium incentives	39	-
State planning (SMSC)	13	-
Rural CEP's	7	-
Territories	2	-
Total	203	-
Balance (carried over Fiscal 1976)	23	-

Source: Manpower Administration, U. S. Dept. of Labor
a/ Percent of funds for comparable manpower programs.
b/ Adjusted to provide each prime sponsor at least 90 per-
    cent but not more than 150 percent of prior year's funds.

received at least 90 percent of their prior year's funding
level. The regional shifts are about the same as those
under the formula amount.

The basic reason for the geographic shift in distribution of funds is the fact that the Title I formula places
three times as much weight on unemployment as on low
income. Distribution of pre-CETA funds was based to
a greater extent on poverty or other factors. States
that have experienced the greatest losses based on the
CETA formula before the 90 percent adjustment are

Table 5. Percent Distribution of Manpower Funds, Fiscal Year 1974 and Fiscal Year 1975, by State Quintiles Based on Amount of Funds in Fiscal Year 1974

Quintile of States by Amount of Funds in FY 1974[a]	FY 1974 Manpower Funds[b]	FY 1975 Title I Allocation[c]	
		Formula Amount	Adjusted Amount[d]
1 (Most funds)	52. 8	54. 6	54. 2
2	22. 1	21. 1	21. 4
3	14. 8	13. 9	14. 3
4	7. 4	7. 4	7. 2
5	2. 9	3. 0	2. 9
ALL STATES	100. 0	100. 0	100. 0

Source: Computed from Manpower Administration data
a/ Puerto Rico and D. C. omitted.
b/ Funds for programs corresponding with Title I.
c/ Excludes consortium incentives, State funds for manpower services, vocational education, and planning, funds for rural CEP's and for Guam, Virgin Islands, Samoa, and Trust Territories.
d/ Adjusted to provide each prime sponsor at least 90 percent but not more than 150 percent of prior year's funds.

those where the ratio of adults in low-income families to the number of unemployed persons is high. Correspondingly, states that have gained (or decreased the least) tend to be those with low ratios of adults in low-income families to unemployed persons. Table 7 shows the distribution of states by percent change in funds from 1974. States that gained most relative to other states averaged 5. 1 adults in low-income families for each unemployed person. Those in the lowest group had a 13. 5 to 1 ratio.[16]

16/ The correlation of the rank of states by percent change in funds from 1974 and the rank by the poverty/unemployment ratio, using the Spearman method is $\rho = .67$.

Table 6. Percent Distribution and Relative Change of
Manpower Funds Fiscal Year 1974 and Fiscal Year 1975,
by Region

Census Region	Percent Distribution			Percent FY 1975 Allocation of FY 1974 Funds	
	Fiscal Year 1974 Manpower Funds[a/]	Fiscal Year 1975 Title I Allocation[b/]			
		Formula Amount	Adjusted Amount[c/]	Formula Amount	Adjusted Amount
New England	5.9	6.2	6.2	93.3	100.6
Middle Atlantic	17.1	17.3	17.2	90.2	97.2
East North Central	17.4	17.3	17.8	88.3	98.2
West North Central	7.2	6.9	7.0	85.6	93.8
South Atlantic	15.3	14.5	14.8	84.5	93.1
East South Central	7.5	6.7	7.1	79.4	90.6
West South Central	10.0	9.6	9.6	85.5	91.6
Mountain	4.5	4.3	4.3	84.9	93.1
Pacific	12.3	14.0	13.2	100.7	103.1
Alaska, Hawaii, Puerto Rico	2.9	3.2	3.0	97.5	99.2
ALL REGIONS	100.0	100.0	100.0	88.8	96.2

Source: Computed from Manpower Administration data

a/ Funds for programs corresponding with Title I.
b/ Excludes consortium incentives, special State funds,
   funds for rural CEP's and for Territories.
c/ Adjusted to provide each prime sponsor at least 90
   but not more than 150 percent of prior year's funds.

Table 7.　Low-income Adults/Unemployment Ratio, by State Quintiles based on Relative Change in Manpower Funds From Fiscal Year 1974 to Fiscal Year 1975, Title I

Quintile of States by Relative Change in FY 1975 Formula Allocation Compared with FY 1974 Manpower Funds[a/]	Low-Income Adults/ Unemployment Ratio
1 (Most change)	5. 1
2	5. 8
3	7. 6
4	10. 3
5	13. 5
ALL STATES	7. 6

Source:　Computed from Manpower Administration data
a/　Puerto Rico and D. C. omitted.

　　In other words, states whose economic problems are characterized by low income rather than unemployment were relative losers under the CETA Title I formula because of the low weight given to the income factor.

Type of Sponsor

　　The relative effect of the CETA Title I formula distribution is to shift funds from cities to counties. The amounts going to consortia, which combine cities, counties, and smaller jurisdictions, and the balance-of-state funds remain relatively unchanged compared with the previous year (Table 8). After the minimum and maximum adjustments are made, changes from the previous year are less pronounced.

　　Changes from the fiscal 1974 base by type of sponsor show that counties in the aggregate would have received 107 percent of their base amount (Table 9), but cities would have received only 77 percent of their base

Table 8.   Percent Distribution of Manpower Funds,
Fiscal Year 1974 and Fiscal Year 1975, by Type of
Sponsor

Type of Sponsor	Fiscal Year 1974 Manpower Funds[a]/	Fiscal Year 1975 Title I Allocation[b]/	
		Formula Amount	Adjusted Amount[c]/
City	25. 1	21. 7	23. 6
County	13. 5	16. 3	15. 1
Consortium	30. 6	30. 6	30. 9
Balance of State	30. 8	31. 5	30. 4
ALL SPONSORS	100. 0	100. 0	100. 0

Source: Computed from Manpower Administration data
a/   Funds for programs corresponding with Title I.
b/   Excludes consortium incentives, State funds for manpower services, vocational education, and planning,
funds for rural CEP's and for Guam, Virgin Islands,
Samoa, and Trust Territories.
c/   Adjusted to provide each prime sponsor at least 90
percent but not more than 150 percent of prior year's
funds.
(Details may not add to totals due to rounding.)

amounts.   The adjustments again tended to flatten the
differences.

    There are several cities whose funds would amount
to less than 70 percent of their fiscal 1974 level were it
not for the hold-harmless factor; only a few cities would
receive more than 100 percent of their fiscal 1974 amount.
On the other hand, only one county and two consortia
would receive less than 70 percent.

    A closer look at the distributive effects of the CETA
Title I formula was obtained by disaggregating consortium
funds among component jurisdictions.   Fiscal 1974 funds
and 1975 Title I formula amounts for cities or counties
of 100, 000 or more were added to the city or county totals
respectively.   Funds for smaller jurisdictions were assigned to the balance-of-state category.   The results
show approximately the same pattern of relative change
as that shown in Table 8.   The share going to cities

Table 9. Percent Fiscal Year 1975 of Fiscal Year 1974
Manpower Funds, by Type of Sponsor

Type of Sponsor	Percent FY 1975 Title I Allocation[a] of FY 1974 Manpower Funds[b]			
	Formula Amount		Adjusted Amount[c]	
	Range	Average	Range	Average
City	53-180	77	90-150	90
County	68-292	107	90-150	108
Consortium	63-143	89	90-134	97
Balance of State	70-127	91	90-127	95
ALL SPONSORS	53-292	89	90-150	96

Source: Computed from Manpower Administration data

a/ Excludes consortium incentives, State funds for man-
    power services, vocational education, and planning,
    funds for rural CEP's and for Guam, Virgin Islands,
    Samoa, and Trust Territories.
b/ Funds for programs corresponding with Title I.
c/ Adjusted to provide each prime sponsor at least 90
    percent but not more than 150 percent of prior year's
    funds.

declined sharply from that of fiscal 1974, counties received relatively more, while the balance-of-states
share increased slightly:

Type of Sponsor	Fiscal Year 1974 Manpower Funds (percent)	Fiscal Year 1975 Title I Formula Allocation (percent)
City	41.9	36.1
County	21.2	25.6
Balance of State	36.8	38.3
	100.0	100.0

The redistribution of funds among types of prime
sponsors reflects the influence of all three elements in
the formula. The first (weighted 50 percent) was new

obligations for fiscal 1974. The amounts for this factor were estimated by regional offices based on contracts
and grants for MDTA and EOA programs in 1974.[17]/

The second and third factors--number of unemployed
and number of adults in low-income families--influenced
the change in the funding pattern. If unemployment were
the sole measure of need, about 20 percent of the pie
would go to counties. If low income were the sole criterion, counties would get 14 percent, and the lion's
share would go to the balance of state programs, which
are heavily rural (Table 10).

Table 10. Percent Distribution Fiscal Year 1974 and
Fiscal Year 1975 Manpower Funds Compared with Hypothetical Allocations, by Type of Sponsor

Type of Sponsor	FY 1974 Manpower Funds[a]/	FY 1975 Formula Alloca-tion[b]/	Hypothetical FY 1975 Formula Allocation Based On	
			Unemploy-ment	Adults in Low Income Families
City	25.1	21.7	19.4	14.8
County	13.5	16.3	20.6	14.4
Consortium	30.6	30.6	30.9	29.6
Balance of State	30.8	31.5	29.2	41.1
ALL SPONSORS	100.0	100.0	100.0	100.0

Source: Computed from Manpower Administration data
a/ Funds for programs corresponding with Title I.
b/ Excludes consortium incentives, State funds for manpower services, vocational education, and planning,
   funds for rural CEP's and for Territories.
(Details may not add to totals due to rounding.)

The distributive effect of the formula between cities
and adjacent suburbs is demonstrated by the following
example for the Minneapolis-St. Paul metropolitan area
(Table 11).

17/ Manpower Administration Field Memorandum No.
    29-74, February 6, 1974.

Table 11.   Percent Distribution of Fiscal Year 1974 and
Fiscal Year 1975 Manpower Funds by Component Sections
of Minneapolis-St. Paul Standard Metropolitan Statistical
Area[a]/

City or County	FY 1974 Manpower Funds[b]/	1973 Unem- ployed	Adults in Low- Income Families	FY 1975 Title I Allocation[c]/	
				Formula Amount	Adjusted Amount[d]/
Minneapolis	50.9	30.6	37.5	40.2	46.3
St. Paul	29.6	19.1	23.1	24.1	26.9
Bal. of Hennepin County	6.3	23.3	18.1	15.3	9.5
Bal. of Ramsey County	3.6	7.6	5.9	5.7	4.8
Anoka County	4.3	9.2	5.8	6.8	5.7
Dakota County	3.4	6.2	5.8	4.9	4.1
Washington County	2.0	4.1	3.9	3.2	2.7
TOTAL	100.0	100.0	100.0	100.0	100.0

Source: Computed from Manpower Administration data
a/ Old definition.
b/ Funds for programs corresponding with Title I.
c/ Excludes consortium incentives, State funds for man-
    power services, vocational education, and planning,
    funds for rural CEP's and for Guam, Virgin Islands,
    Samoa, and Trust Territories.
d/ Adjusted to provide each prime sponsor at least 90
    percent but not more than 150 percent of prior year's
    funds.
(Details may not add to totals due to rounding.)

        Included in the Minneapolis-St. Paul area, was
that part of Hennepin County outside the central city,
estimated to have received only 6.3 percent of manpower

funds for the standard metropolitan statistical area[18]/
(SMSA) in 1974. However, its volume of unemployment
would have justified 23.3 percent, and if adults in low-
income families were the sole criterion, the county
would have received 18.1 percent. The county actually
wound up under the Title I allocation with 9.5 percent of
the SMSA funds--a gain from 6.3 percent in the previous
year but less than the amount warranted by unemployment and poverty figures.

In sum, the Title I formula produced a change from
the previous year's distribution pattern despite its stabilizers. Big city prime sponsors who suffered losses
compared with 1974, and who face further erosion of
funds in coming years, complain that they are being
treated unfairly. County prime sponsors, on the other
hand, argue that they had been shortchanged in the past
and that CETA will eventually bring them closer to
parity with cities.

The fundamental issue of what is fair and equitable
in distributing resources depends on the objectives of
Title I. In allotting a significant proportion (37.5 percent) of the funds on the basis of the number of unemployed, no distinction is made between a temporarily
unemployed skilled worker who may have substantial
resources and good prospects for reemployment, and a
severely disadvantaged person. In periods of robust
economic growth, the disadvantaged constitute a relatively high percentage of total unemployment. Under
these conditions, allocations based on unemployment
may more fairly reflect the needs of the disadvantaged.
However, in recessionary periods, it is questionable
whether unemployment is a satisfactory measure of the
hard-core unemployed for whom manpower programs
prior to CETA were intended. This raises the question
as to whether more refined formulas for different program objectives and target groups are needed.

The issue of funding distribution may become more
serious. About 40 percent of the prime sponsors required

18/ A standard metropolitan statistical area is an integrated economic and social unit with a large population nucleus, as defined by the Office of Management
and Budget.

discretionary funds in 1975 to sustain them close to the
prior year's funding level. Seventy-eight percent of the
cities and 53 percent of the consortia were in this group
(not counting consortium incentive funds). They face
the prospect of diminishing funds over several years,
while the formula tends to increase amounts going to
other sponsors. This will increase pressure on cities
especially, unless additional funds are continuously
pumped into CETA. Meanwhile the Administration's
fiscal 1976 budget requests the same amount of Title I
funds as in 1975 ($1. 6 billion) and again omits summer
youth programs. [19]/

SUMMARY

Analysis of the amount and the manner of allocating
funds reveals the following aspects of manpower policy
and resource allocation.

- The sharp rise in funds from the early 1960s to
  the present reflects the growing recognition of
  the importance of manpower programs.
- The amount of funds available under CETA ($3. 7
  billion in 1975) is a substantial increase over
  1974 funding for comparable manpower programs.
  However, most of the gain is for public service
  employment and for summer youth programs.
  The amount for comprehensive manpower programs (Title I) is 12 percent higher than the
  amount for comparable programs in 1974.
- From the mid-1960s emphasis had been on structural problems: training and employability development of the disadvantaged. In the early
  1970s emphasis had begun to shift toward cyclical
  problems with a large share of funds devoted to
  public service employment.

[19]/ The practice of holding the lid on spending each year
and restoring funds for summer youth programs later
creates problems for planning and inefficiencies in
administration.

- Although CETA is intended to be a decategorized program, more than half of the funds appropriated are specifically earmarked. However, nearly 90 percent of the funds are now administered by local and state prime sponsors.
- The emphasis on formula methods of distributing funds is a marked departure from the past. Allocation formulas are prescribed for most of the CETA funds (Titles I, II, and VI). Previously, manpower funds were largely distributed on the basis of various concepts of need. The use of a formula introduces objective methods of allotment and universalizes the distribution of funds.
- The distributional effects of the Title I formula are:

    1) Funds during the first year were shifted from the South to the West and the Northeast, from states with relatively high poverty populations to those with relatively more unemployment.

    2) There has been a relative shift from cities to counties: consortia and balance-of-state funds on the whole maintain about the same share of funds as in the base year. Changes have been mitigated during the first year by the built-in stabilizers; cities, particularly, benefited from the 90 percent hold-harmless factor in the first year. In each successive year, the amount going to cities will continue to decrease unless total funding increases.

- The main reason for the distributional change is the heavy reliance on the unemployment element in the formula as contrasted with the poverty element. The choice of a $7,000 low-income cutoff, rather than the standard poverty criterion, tends to limit the influence of the low-income factor as a measure of economic need.

3

Manpower Planning

Under the new manpower law, state or local prime sponsors are required to draw up comprehensive plans for furnishing manpower services, which must be approved by the federal government before funding. The act also requires local planning councils to be set up to analyze needs and to recommend goals, policies, and procedures. Chapter 3 examines the impact of CETA on the planning system in terms of extent of community and local government participation in the planning process, changes in activities of planning councils and in decision making, and the effectiveness of the present planning system for the administration of programs.

PLANNING BEFORE CETA

The realization that manpower programs were multiplying with little design or coordination in the 1960s led to efforts to bring some order out of the chaotic situation by means of an area manpower planning system. In 1967 the Cooperative Area Manpower Planning System (CAMPS) was introduced. Systematic planning in a community, based upon an analysis of the needs of special groups for manpower services, was assumed to result in appropriate programs and a rational allocation of available resources.

To accomplish this, CAMPS provided for a national committee consisting of representatives of federal agencies administering manpower or related programs, supplemented by a network of counterpart committees at regional, state, and local levels. Local committees, originally established for major Standard Metropolitan Statistical Areas were later set up for smaller areas. Local plans were consolidated at the state level and forwarded to regional planning committees. In the formative years, committee membership was confined to public agencies; community participation was nonexistent. Participation was voluntary and public agencies with no direct operational role soon lost interest.

CAMPS planning started with the organization of demographic and labor market data to furnish a framework for analyzing a community's manpower needs. The resulting plans were not completely comprehensive; only manpower programs funded by the Department of Labor were included. For the most part, the early CAMPS system was a means of exchanging information rather than a meaningful planning process in itself. Committees were not regarded as influential in the allocation of resources.

In the early 1970s an attempt was made to shift some responsibility for local program decisions from federal to local government. In 1971 CAMPS was restructured to provide for three levels of planning: a State Manpower Planning Council (SMPC) under the governor, an Area Manpower Planning Council (AMPC) under officials of the largest city in each CAMPS area, and an Ancillary Manpower Planning Board (AMPB) for a planning district in the balance of the state. The Manpower Administration's policy guides for 1972 were clearly intended to continue the move toward decentralization by increasing the responsibility of state and local officials and by providing for more flexible funding of manpower programs. The change did not remove federal responsibility for specific decisions, yet it did move the planning process into a new stage: local recommendations were now to be taken into account. To infuse more life into this system, state and local officials were given funds to hire planning staffs. By 1974 every state, 160 cities, and 161 counties had operational planning grants.

Fiscal 1974 marked a milestone in the movement toward decentralization. CAMPS instructions for that year introduced the term manpower revenue-sharing program. The Manpower Administration announced that local officials would be given more leeway in making recommendations for the use of fiscal 1974 funds of MDTA and EOA by means of area plans. However, the extent to which regional offices followed local recommendations in allocating resources has never been fully documented.

The Nixon Administration had embraced the concept of New Federalism and was pushing vigorously for manpower revenue-sharing legislation. Without the support of such legislation it opted to move administratively as far as possible toward decentralization. The Manpower Administration began by establishing pilot decentralized programs known as comprehensive manpower programs in nine areas and proposed to add more. Legislative events overtook these attempts at decentralization; by December 1973, Congress had enacted CETA and the move toward revenue-sharing under existing authority was quietly abandoned as all efforts were redirected toward implementation of the new law.

The experience of various communities in manpower planning was mixed. Some areas had developed meaningful planning capability, but for most, manpower planning remained a token exercise. Nevertheless, cumulative experience, especially the funding of some 1200 planning positions in state, city, and county governments, laid the groundwork for a transition to a more comprehensive local planning system. Pre-CETA planning experience, at the very least, developed a core of manpower planners and brought about some communication among manpower agencies at the local level. To that extent it facilitated the planning process under CETA.

CETA emphasizes local planning as an essential component of a decentralized program. The act requires the establishment of local manpower planning councils to advise on needs for service, program plans, basic goals, and policies and procedures, as well as to monitor employment and training programs. Considerable local input was intended although final decision making is reserved

for the prime sponsor. In addition to the manpower
planning council, the act establishes the State Manpower
Services Council (SMSC) as advisor to the governor to
review and coordinate local plans, to monitor programs,
and to issue an annual report.

THE GEOGRAPHY OF CETA PLANNING

The geographic unit for manpower planning has usually been an economically integrated labor market area.
Despite inducements to form voluntary interjurisdictional
arrangements, CETA has in effect broken up planning
areas into smaller geographic units. This development,
of course, was the consequence of designating political
units of government as prime sponsors; it both helps and
hinders the planning process. The use of smaller political units ties planning more closely to the political
structure of cities and counties, enabling planners to
focus on a more homogeneous target population. However,
a smaller area tends to separate the place of work from
the place of residence, thus limiting access to employment opportunities. Smaller planning units also make
cooperation among jurisdictions in the use of facilities
for manpower services more difficult.

Sixteen of the 24 local prime sponsors in the study
sample are smaller than labor market areas. Kansas
City (Kan.), for example, was splintered off from a bi-
state SMSA. Since most employment opportunities are
in Missouri, while a disproportionate number of the disadvantaged live in Kansas, effective program planning
and coordination was constrained. Similarly, in Union
County (N. J.), the prime sponsor area was cut off from
a major employment center in Elizabeth, thus limiting
the use of facilities and affecting job development.

Type of Sponsor	Area same as or larger than SMSA	Area Smaller than SMSA
City	0	6
County	3	6
Consortium	5	4
	8	16

Despite these problems, most local prime sponsors in the study sample believe that the planning system can be adjusted to a smaller and more unified area. Some note that a smaller area may be more realistic for disadvantaged urban residents, whose commuting range is limited by inadequate public transportation. Generally, it is felt that labor market considerations are less compelling than institutional and political considerations.

PLANNING COUNCIL ORGANIZATION

The fact that a CAMPS system existed, that manpower planners were funded in some cities and counties before CETA, and that some local public officials began to be involved in planning prior to CETA made the transition easier in most instances. However, the changeover to CETA significantly affected the structure of the planning system in terms of areas covered and planning resources.

The most immediate impact of CETA has been the extension of the planning system to jurisdictions not previously involved, and to integrate planning staffs into the structure of state and local governments. On the whole, planning systems are becoming institutionalized to a greater extent than before. The framework is being reshaped to enlarge local participation in decision making.

Of the 24 local prime sponsors, five are establishing planning systems for the first time (Table 12). Those sponsors are mainly in suburbs or satellite cities and counties that had been part of a larger area and so only peripherally involved in planning. Without benefit of planning council, staff, or plan, these five sponsors began to establish planning systems. Cook County (Ill.), for example, had been part of the Chicago MAPC. Under CETA, the County became an independent prime sponsor, formed its own council, and hired its own planning staff.

A second group of five prime sponsors had only minimal contact with planning before CETA. Although each of those areas had been the central city or county of a pre-CETA manpower planning area, little planning was done; there was no planning staff. Such plans as did exist had been made by the State Manpower Planning

Table 12. Relationship of Sample Local Prime Sponsor
Planning Structure to Pre-CETA Planning Structure

Type of Sponsor	Local Prime Sponsors[a]/	Same Planning Structure as Pre-CETA	Different from Pre-CETA Central City or County of Pre-CETA Planning Area		Suburb or Satellite of Pre-CETA Area
			With Planning Staff	Without Planning Staff	
City	6	2	3	0	1
County	9	1	1	3	4
Consortium	9	6	1	2	0
TOTAL	24	9	5	5	5

a/ Excluding balance of States.

Council or by the local employment service. For all intents and purposes the prime sponsors also created new planning structures. The Pinellas-St. Petersburg (Fla.) Consortium faced this problem. Before CETA, Pinellas County was the central part of a three-county AMPB. However, since the pre-CETA plan was prepared at the state level for the AMPB, there was virtually no local planning experience when the prime sponsor took over.

Five other prime sponsors, each of whose jurisdictions was formerly the central city or county of either an MAPC or an AMPB, were able to make the transition more readily since they already had staffs, councils, and plans. Middlesex County (N. J.), now a prime sponsor in its own right, is typical of this situation. Before CETA, Middlesex was the dominant partner in a two-county AMPB. A small staff with some experience was a link between the old and new planning systems.

The remaining nine prime sponsors of the survey sample were in an even more favorable position. Each of their CETA areas coincided with a former MAPC or AMPB, and council, staff, and plans were already in

place.   The large cities in the sample--New York and
Philadelphia--and most of the consortia are in this
category.   In New York City, although the planning council had been virtually inactive for a year, there was sufficient expertise available to begin planning under CETA.
In another case, planning staff in the office of the mayor
of Santa Ana, the principal city of the Orange County
Consortium (Cal.), became the nucleus for planning and
administration under CETA.   Thus, most of the local
prime sponsors were in a position to build their planning
around an existing MAPC or AMPB, although frequently
these groups were relatively inactive.

Appreciable staff increases accompanied the expanding manpower planning systems and the growth is continuing.   Fourteen of the 24 local prime sponsor
jurisdictions had some planning staff resources before
CETA.   In the remaining 10 areas, plans were drawn up
either by a planning staff of the central city, by the employment service, or by the State Manpower Planning
Council staff.   Now all areas have their own staffs,
which, unlike the pre-CETA situation, are integrated
with the personnel responsible for program administration.[20]/

Typically under CETA, one or more persons is identified as manpower planner, but in practice, except in
the largest jurisdictions, they have additional responsibilities.   In some cases they work closely with members
or subcommittees of the planning council.   When this occurs, they are responsible to the manpower administrator
rather than the council.   Planning is thus becoming institutionalized as an essential component of the CETA administrator's staff and closely tied in with the administrative
process.

COMPOSITION OF LOCAL PLANNING COUNCILS

The framers of CETA viewed the local advisory
council as the vehicle through which broad participation

[20]/ However, in New York City the planning staff is
       assigned to the executive director of the Council,
       and is not part of the CETA Administrator's office.

in manpower activities could be realized. They carefully specified its membership: representatives of client
groups, community-based organizations, the employment
service, education and training agencies and institutions,
business, labor, and where appropriate, agriculture.

The study found the composition of councils little
changed from that of their predecessors. The key differences are in the control of council activities and the
participation of council members. New alignments in
the power structure and rearrangements of the patterns
of influence are surfacing. The dominance of the traditional manpower service agencies is on the wane and is
being replaced by the CETA administrator and staff.
Elected officials are also taking a greater interest in
planning and decision making.

The typical local CETA manpower planning council
in the study sample has 24 members. The program operators (the employment service, education and training
institutions, and community-based organizations) comprise 30 percent of total membership (Table 13). Another
large group of members is made up of other public officials including elected officials or their representatives.
In New York City, to take an extreme case, 28 or 40
council members are either program operators or part
of the CETA administration. Client groups represent
about one-fifth of the local council membership in all
areas, and business and labor together comprise almost
one-fourth.

In areas where geographic coverage changed, the
size and composition of planning councils was modified
from that of earlier committees. Prime sponsors whose
areas are now smaller have dropped representatives of
outlying cities or counties. Where there was a shift of
control from cities to the county (as in Union County,
N. J.) the change was reflected in the composition of the
councils.

To assess changes attributable to CETA, areas with
similar geographic boundaries before and after CETA
were examined. In some of these 13 cases the pre-CETA
council was retained without change. In Philadelphia,
St. Paul, Topeka, and Cleveland, for example, the CETA
council is virtually the same as the MAPC. For the

Table 13.   Composition of Sample Local Prime Sponsor
Planning Councils Fiscal Year 1975, and Comparison
with Pre-CETA Councils

Organizations or Groups Represented	Percent Distribution		
	Local Prime Sponsors (N=23)[a]	Matched Planning Areas[b]	
		Pre-CETA (N=13)	CETA (N=13)
Employment Service	5	7	6
Education/ training agency	13	15	13
Other public agencies	18	20	22
Community-based organizations	11	13	12
Client Groups	21	17	17
Labor	9	8	8
Business/ industry	14	10	13
Other	9	10	9
ALL GROUPS	100	100	100

a/ Data for one sample area not available.
b/ Sample prime sponsor areas with comparable size
     before and under CETA.
(Note: figures are averages of percentages.)

sample of 13 as a whole, the proportion of service deliverers (employment service, vocational education, and
community-based organizations) appears to be slightly
lower than in CAMPS (31 percent vs 35 percent).
     The proportion of employment service and educa-
tional representatives on CETA councils, slightly smaller than formerly, reflects a conscious effort of prime
sponsors to broaden representation.   The employment

service offices had tended to dominate the CAMPS councils; they supplied basic data needed for plans, determined the training needs, and often provided the planning staff. The leading role began to shift away from the employment service even before CETA, with the hiring of planning staffs for local MAPCs and for State Manpower Planning Councils.

Under CETA the influence of the employment service has continued to decline in most of the sample areas as the CETA administrator's role has increased. In Lorain County (Oh.), for example, an employment service official formerly chaired the AMPB and provided labor market information and other data for plans. Under CETA the employment service is on the council but the administrator dominates its activities.

The composition of planning councils to some extent reflects relationships of member organizations to the power structure. Predictably, the proportion of client groups and community-based organizations to total urban council membership is high, nearly half of the membership, but it is only about one-fourth of county councils. On the other hand, education and other public officials are more prominent in county and consortia councils than in those of cities (Table 14).

The influence and activity of community-based organizations in planning has increased in several of the cities in the sample since control over resources has shifted from federal to local authorities. In counties and consortia, however, community-action agencies and other community-based organizations are less influential and have encountered problems. In the San Joaquin (Cal.) and Phoenix consortia, community-based organizations that operate programs are not members of the council because of possible conflicts of interest. In the Raleigh (N. C.) Consortium, the major community-action agency was permitted to be on the council only after a protest had been lodged with the regional office of the Manpower Administration. In Lorain (Oh.) and Chester (Pa.) Counties, community-action agencies were initially overlooked. Client representation has been a controversial issue in only a few places. In Long Beach (Cal.) and New York, blacks felt they were underrepresented; there were

Table 14.   Composition of Sample Local Prime Sponsor
Planning Councils, by Type of Sponsor, Fiscal Year
1975[a]/

Organizations or Groups Represented	Percent Distribution		
	City (N=6)	County (N=9)	Consortium (N=8)[a]/
Employment service	4	6	6
Education/training agency	8	14	15
Other public agencies	7	24	21
Community-based organizations	16	7	11
Client groups	31	19	15
Labor	11	8	7
Business/industry	13	16	14
Other	10	6	11
ALL GROUPS	100	100	100

[a]/ Data for one sample area not available.
(Note: figures are averages of percentages.)

complaints as well from Puerto Ricans in New York and
from a Chicano group in St. Paul.

COUNCIL FUNCTIONS

Activities of pre-CETA councils, it is generally
agreed, were limited to an exchange of information and
recommendations for funding. MAPCs acted in an advisory capacity to mayors, who (in 1974) forwarded funding
recommendations to the regional office of the Manpower
Administration. AMPBs transmitted recommendations
through State Manpower Planning Councils. Decision
making, however, remained with the Department of
Labor, which was not obliged to follow the proposals.
Pre-CETA councils had no responsibility for administration

or evaluation of programs and had little impact on decision making.

With new legislation in the wind, interim councils and task forces were appointed to shape up realistic plans in anticipation of local control. The mayor of St. Paul appointed an interim council early in 1973 to make recommendations for 1974. That group evolved into the CETA planning council, and their work provided the basis for the Title I comprehensive manpower plan. In New York, although the area planning council was not functioning when CETA was passed, some of its members, mostly from city government agencies, were hastily assembled to whip up a Title I plan. Later the council was revived and designated as the CETA council. In the San Joaquin Consortium, early CAMPS plans were dusted off and used to prepare the Title I plan. The Area Manpower Planning Council, which prior to 1973 had been ineffectual, came alive when the city of Stockton became the sponsor and funding source for a number of programs in 1974. In the Lansing area, a technical planning council, composed of local manpower program officials who met regularly before CETA, acted as a transitional council.

The survey evidence suggests that most of the CETA councils played little or no role in preparing 1975 Title I plans. Inadequate time was the most frequent explanation. Several of the local manpower advisory committees were not yet functioning. When the committees were operative, Title I plans generally were pulled together hastily by the CETA administrator's staff for approval by the planning councils. In New York, for example, a council meeting was called in June 1974 to approve the Title I plan, and no further meetings were held until December 1974. Even in Gary (Ind.), where the MAPC committee was carried over as the CETA council, the Title I plan was developed essentially by the staff of the manpower administrator based on past experience, and was cleared through the planning council without much participation by members. Phoenix prepared its Title I plan before the appointment of the planning council. However, some of these councils began to function more actively in connection with Title II and Title VI plans.

The Lansing Consortium manpower planning council, appointed in January 1975, met in February to consider a Title VI plan.

Eight councils did make a significant contribution to the Title I plan either as a full council or through subcommittees. The Chester County (Pa.) Council, at the initiative of the CETA administrator, became involved early in allocation of resources and determination of programs, as well as in administrative and program problems. These activities contrast sharply with the activities of the pre-CETA council in that County.

The role and style of CETA councils are shaped by the relationships among the CETA administrator, the staff, and the council members. Some hold regularly scheduled formal meetings, others operate more informally, with CETA staff consulting with individual council members or subcommittees. In San Joaquin, for example, the planning and evaluation subcommittee is actively involved in planning, but the rest of the council is relatively inactive.

Although the style of council operations varies widely, in most cases the council depends upon the staff for planning, review of project proposals, and preparation of the planning document. In nearly all cases, the CETA administrator and staff play a commanding role in council affairs.

The scope of the CETA councils' activities, dealing with the entire range of operations, and the direct relationship of CETA councils to the decision makers distinguishes the councils from their predecessors. However, the CETA manpower planning council is still essentially an advisory body.

DECISION MAKING

Congress, recognizing that decentralization required the vesting of decision making authority with the prime sponsor, made an effort to provide local groups with an opportunity to participate in the process. To afford an avenue for such participation the legislators mandated advisory councils, which they clearly intended to be more than window dressing.

The decision-making process under CETA is complex, and opinions differ as to where the balance of power lies in the formal local CETA structure: with the council, the CETA administrator, the staff, or the elected officials.

In four of the 24 local areas surveyed the manpower planning councils appear to have the key role in decision making in the first planning cycle. The Pinellas-St. Petersburg Consortium is one of these. There the planning process is described as a continuous interrelationship among staff, local elected officials, program operators, and client group representatives. Decisions are made by vote of the manpower planning council, and all such decisions have been accepted by the county executive and the CETA administrator.

More typically, councils are merely advisory. However, with the shift of authority to state and local officials, councils are closer to the seat of power and can exercise a more direct influence than was possible under MAPCs or AMPBs, especially where councils operate through subcommittees.

The interplay of forces within the council becomes important in decision making. In some cases the executive committee appears to have considerable weight; in others, group alignments along interest lines may be influential. For example, coalitions of community-based organizations may be formed or alliances may develop along geographic lines.

The question of whether CETA administrators make final decisions that are formally confirmed by elected officials, or whether elected officials themselves make decisions is difficult to assess. Typically, the CETA administrator reports formally to the city or county executive or to a consortium board. Informally, however, the extent of decision making by the elected official depends on personal perceptions of the importance of manpower programs and the relative reliance on the CETA administrator.

In large jurisdictions, the mayor or board of commissioners delegates responsibility for planning to administrative officials. In other jurisdictions, elected officials are in closer touch with the manpower program

and more likely to enter directly into decision making.
The survey revealed a few situations in which elected
officials chair the council or are members of it.   More
commonly, the CETA administrator provides the con=
necting link with council activities.   In Middlesex and
Union Counties, for example, members of the Board
of Freeholders actively participate in council deliberations; this helps ensure concurrence of the board with
council decisions.   In consortia, decisions are often
made formally by a board or executive committee consisting of elected officials or their designees.   However,
the informal mechanisms depend largely upon relationships between the board and the CETA staff.   On the
whole, the present situation is a sharp contrast to the
pre-CETA picture, in which the elected official had
little responsibility or interest in manpower planning.

     With their new CETA role, many elected officials
are becoming aware of manpower problems and programs
in their communities.   But there is no evidence that the
public at large is becoming more involved in the planning
process, either indirectly through elected officials or
directly through participation on councils.

     The attention focused on unemployment has made
manpower programs, particularly the amount of funds
available for Title VI jobs, front page news, yet CETA
administrators report virtually no reaction or participation in the planning process by the community at large.
All prime sponsors complied with federal regulations
regarding publication of Title I plans or summaries of
them, usually by notice in local newspapers.   In a few
cases the public was invited to attend meetings of the advisory council while it considered the plan.   Observers
report little response to these formal steps.   Few people
attended the public hearings, and rarely did anyone ask
to see the plan.

     Some observers noted that the decision-making pro-
cess has not yet been tested.   In many areas, funding
was equal to or more than the amount available in fiscal
1974.   Consequently, hard decisions involving cutbacks in
manpower programs have not been necessary.   Conditions
resulting from the economic downturn, availability of
funds under Title VI, and the need for vast readjustments

in Title I plans are bringing manpower councils closer
to the decision-making process.

DEVELOPING THE PLANNING DOCUMENT

The art of manpower planning had progressed before
CETA. Labor market and demographic data were com-
piled by employment service analysts for local plans.
However, the plans lacked evaluative data and often did
not relate programs to economic data. To a large extent the planning process was considered an exercise
to meet federal requirements.

The CETA plan consists of an analysis of manpower
problems in the area, identification of population groups
in need of assistance, description of the proposed activities, arrangements to deliver these services, and the
results that may be expected.

Plans prepared for Title I grants were oriented
mainly to immediate administrative requirements and
did not constitute planning in a more strategic sense.
In areas in which CETA prime sponsors used experienced planning staffs, Title I plans tended to be mere
extensions of earlier plans.

In some cases, however, plans developed in anticipation of manpower revenue-sharing were converted to
CETA plans with contributions from CETA administrators
or councils regarding goals, priorities, types of programs,
and groups in need of services. In Austin, for example,
a comprehensive plan previously turned down by the regional office was resubmitted as the Title I plan. St. Paul
staff members had a novel plan and were waiting for an
opportunity to put it into effect.

In areas lacking planning experience, the development of a Title I plan was difficult. In Stanislaus County
(Cal.), for instance, the seven-county pre-CETA AMPB
plan was prepared by state staff in Sacramento. Nobody
in the county had a clear idea of where to obtain data.
The CETA planner had to seek information from the employment service, the Chamber of Commerce, school
districts, and city and county planning departments.

Putting together a Title I plan was not a thorough
job in most cases. There was little time for analysis

by staff, or for review and input by manpower planning councils. Economic data were seldom integrated with the program operations plan. Regional offices of the Manpower Administration found serious technical deficiencies in most plans, and many were returned repeatedly for further work.

CETA administrators were asked to comment on the usefulness of labor market information and demographic data in the preparation of the planning document. Most felt that such information was of limited use in identifying groups in need of manpower services or occupations for training. Some felt that such data were typical federal boiler plate requirements. In any event, past experience in operating programs and gut reactions appeared to be more important in reaching decisions than the availability of statistical profiles. However, the upsurge in unemployment has made those with planning responsibility more aware of the connection between labor market information and program planning. Title I plans prepared early in 1974 have been reexamined in the context of a looser labor market with fewer openings for on-the-job training and for placement of skill-training graduates.

Since prime sponsor funding is significantly affected by the level of unemployment in an area, elected officials and CETA administrators were vitally concerned with this statistic. A few complained about the validity of unemployment statistics.[21] There was also dissatisfaction over the lack of detailed information on the number of persons needing services. The most common problem, however, was the lack of data that could be used for assessing program operations. Apparently, CETA administrators felt more need for data to measure performance and output than for general types of labor market information.

The most frequently mentioned problem in developing the planning document was insufficient time; others were changes in regulations and data requirements, inexperience of staff and of county or city officials, lack of consultation between the CETA administrative staff

21/ See Chapter 2, pp. 29-30.

and program operators, and the need for building an organizational structure. The latter problem absorbed most of the attention of the staff. As one field research associate put it, "There was so much to do in converting the manpower program system that there was little time for the niceties of planning and analysis." Once again, the urgencies of the moment crowded out the important longer-range considerations.

STATE PLANNING

Under CETA the state government is responsible for two types of manpower advisory councils: the State Manpower Services Council (SMSC) which has a state-wide responsiblity for review, coordination, and monitoring, and the Balance of State manpower planning council (BOS/MPC), which plans for cities and counties with a population of less than 100,000 not covered by a local prime sponsor. The study found that the SMSCs have been ineffective in discharging their responsibilities during the first year because of lack of substantive authority on the part of states under CETA.

In two of the four states in the study sample (Texas and Arizona), separate SMSC and BOS manpower planning councils have been established; in Maine, one council serves both purposes. North Carolina has two councils with considerable overlap in membership. The SMSC is served by a staff unit in the governor's office in Maine and Texas. In Arizona and North Carolina the SMSC as well as the BOS/MPC are assigned to one agency.

	SMSC	BOS/MPC
Maine	Office of Manpower Planning & Coordination Office of Governor	Same
North Carolina	Department of Administration	Same
Texas	Division of Planning Office of Governor	Department of Community Affairs
Arizona	Department of Economic Security	Same

In all four states, prior CAMPS staff were available to help in the transition to CETA and to continue providing technical support to one or both of the councils. The staff were also involved in program administration.

State planning councils are dominated by local and state government officials, who comprise more than 60 percent of the combined membership of the SMSCs and the BOS/MPCs in the four states surveyed. This is understandable, inasmuch as one-third of the membership of SMSCs must be local prime sponsors, and BOS/MPCs include representatives of substate and local jurisdictions. Little controversy has been reported over appointments to state councils except in Maine, where Indian representatives were at first excluded because of their separate funding under Title III; they were later admitted.

The activities of the BOS/MPCs are quite similar to those of their predecessors. The earlier State Manpower Planning Councils channeled local program recommendations to Manpower Administration regional offices; now the BOS/MPCs send their recommendations to their governors. Except in Maine, the BOS/MPCs have delegated the planning responsibility to substate organizations.

In three of the four states studied (Texas, North Carolina, and Maine), the BOS/MPCs contributed little to the planning system during the first year. The Texas council had been inactive until the beginning of 1975, Maine's governor relied on the CETA administrator rather than the council, and in North Carolina the council was appointed too late to make any significant contribution to the Title I plan. Since its appointment, however, the North Carolina council has been involved in decisions regarding service deliverers and has taken a forceful stand in insisting on community participation in the local planning process. The Arizona BOS/MPC did exercise some influence, but the council was not consulted until after the Title I plan had been prepared, under great time pressure, by the planning staff.

With increasing emphasis on decentralization in planning, the future scope of BOS/MPCs may be diminished. In three of the four states surveyed, substate prime sponsors are being established. In these subareas, planning is carried on essentially through the

same mechanisms as before CETA, except in Maine
where the AMPB structure has been bypassed. Substate planning will continue to be based on the Council
of Government or similar structures in Arizona, Texas,
and North Carolina. Generally, these districts, cover-
ing vast distances, do not conform to labor market areas
and have problems using service facilities and matching
job seekers in one part of the district to job opportunities far away. Planners must wrestle with the practical
problems of transportation, selection of training institutions, and scattered populations in rural areas.

The authority and future utility of the SMSC is even
less clear than that of the BOS/MPC. In Texas and
North Carolina the council has concentrated upon recommendations for use of the governor's 4 percent manpower
services fund. Arizona's SMSC planning system has been
developed only recently and its role is still uncertain.
During the early period there was little sign in any of
the four states studied of an effective monitoring or coordinating role. Despite these limiting considerations,
CETA is responsible for the emergence of the governor
or members of his staff in decision making, not only regarding administration, but also in substantive program
questions. Recent unemployment trends have raised the
interest of state as well as local officials in manpower
programs.

SUMMARY

Several points are noteworthy in comparing manpower planning under CETA with earlier planning.

- On the local level, manpower planning has become more universal, more integrated with administration, and closer to the decision makers
  than before.
- CETA has generated greater interest in manpower
  planning on the part of local groups than had previously existed. The predominant influence of
  traditional agencies, particularly the employment
  service, has given way to control by CETA administrators. Elected officials have become

more aware of manpower planning, although the
community at large has not been drawn into the
planning process to any notable extent.

- The decision-making process in manpower planning is complex and depends largely on relationships among the council, the CETA administrator
  and staff, and the elected officials.   Councils are
  generally not the decision-making bodies.   Although elected officials are involved in major issues, they tend to rely largely on the administrative
  and planning staff.   Planning is still essentially a
  bureaucratic rather than a political process, although the nature of the bureaucracy has changed
  under CETA.

- Manpower plans developed under Title I are in
  many cases an outgrowth of earlier plans; more
  than half of all prime sponsor areas had planning
  systems in effect before CETA.   However, there
  was little evidence of planning in any strategic
  sense during the first year because of the urgency
  of drawing up planning documents in support of
  grant applications.

- Most of the local planning councils were not involved in preparation of the Title I plan; many
  were activated much later.   Although still advisory, the scope of CETA council activities is
  considerably broader than that of previous councils.   In many areas, planning is viewed as a
  continuing interaction between advisory councils
  and the CETA administration.   This interaction
  brings more closely together the planning process
  and administrative decisions making each more
  germane to the other.

- The state manpower planning systems are in flux.
  If present trends toward regionalization develop
  further, substate planning groups may increase in
  importance at the expense of BOS/MPCs.   During
  the first cycle, SMSCs did very little to review
  plans, coordinate, or monitor programs.

4

The Administrative Process

The development of manpower programs from their
modest beginnings in the early 1960s was accompanied
by struggles for administrative control at the federal and
local levels. At the national level the conflicts involved
the Department of Labor (DOL), the Department of Health,
Education and Welfare (DHEW), and the Office of Economic
Opportunity (OEO). At the local level various government
and private agencies vied for funding and control of
programs.

The question of who was to administer a coordinated
manpower development system at the state and local
levels if control were to be decentralized had been a
controversial issue for many years.[22/] As early as 1967
an amendment to the EOA assigned the responsibility
for a comprehensive work and training program to local
organizations, most of which were community action
agencies. The 1968 amendments to MDTA gave state
governments the authority to approve all manpower projects funded by the federal government under that act
provided they conformed to an approved state plan. The
implementation of these amendments foundered on

22/ See Robert Guttman, "Intergovernmental Relations
Under the New Manpower Act," Monthly Labor
Review 97(6):10-16, 1974.

bureaucratic shoals and DOL continued to operate categorical manpower programs through the national and
regional offices.

CETA's major achievement--decentralization--
changed relationships among federal, state, and local
levels of government. Local government decision making
and authority to administer programs were enhanced as
the federal role in local programs was diminished. This
set in motion changes at the local level between the prime
sponsor and agencies providing manpower services.
Decentralization was ensured by the designation of state
and local governments as prime sponsors, each with control over a block grant for manpower programs. Local
prime sponsors then faced the herculean task of discharging their new responsibilities while developing a
decentralized manpower system. Their success depends
on how well new roles are defined and accepted and on
how responsibilities are carried out.

Chapter 4 describes the impact of CETA on intergovernmental relationships. It assesses changes in the
administration of manpower programs at all levels of
government, and looks at the effect of CETA on state-
local relationships as well as on interjurisdictional arrangements among local units of government. Most
important, since the shift from federal to local control
is the key to decentralization, changes in the relationships between the regional offices of the Manpower Administration and prime sponsors are examined.

BEFORE CETA

The issues in manpower reform that developed in
the late 1960s were related more to the structure than
to the substance of manpower programs.[23/] The cooperation of DOL and DHEW required by MDTA in 1962 was
one of the earliest experiences in a joint manpower venture. That shotgun marriage was followed by a host of

23/ See Stanley H. Ruttenberg, assisted by Jocelyn
    Gutchess, Manpower Challenge of the 1970s
    (Baltimore: Johns Hopkins Press, 1970).

manpower and antipoverty programs authorized by the
EOA of 1964. The move toward unifying program admin-
istration began at the federal level with the transfer to
DOL of most OEO manpower programs: Neighborhood
Youth Corps, Operation Mainstream, Public Service
Careers, and Job Corps. Within DOL, coordination of
the activities of separate bureaus dealing with manpower
was achieved by the establishment of the Manpower
Administration.

At the local level there was no comparable consolidation of separate programs except in areas where Concentrated Employment Programs (CEPs) were established.
These generally were limited to parts of cities and to a
few rural areas. Before CETA there were several different channels for funding and administering manpower
programs in local areas, but decision making and administration were centralized in the hands of federal authorities in the regional or national office. Most of these
channels bypassed state, county, and city governments.
It was not until the passage of the Emergency Employment
Act (EEA) of 1971 that government units (states, cities
and counties) were given direct control over the funding
and operation of a major manpower program. EEA thus
constituted a stepping stone to the decentralization of
manpower programs.

In the 24 cities, counties, and consortia in the study
sample, control over manpower programs before CETA
was exercised by the Manpower Administration directly
or through state agencies. MDTA training programs were
supervised by state employment service and educational
agencies, which were accountable to federal offices.
Work experience and other programs were supervised by
the Manpower Administration through direct contracts
with schools, community-based organizations, and in
some instances through local governments. Still another
line of control went directly from the national office of
the Manpower Administration to local sponsors. At the
local level there were networks of subcontracts between
CEPs and other program operators.

One effect of the designation of prime sponsors was
to introduce manpower programs into local governments
that had only limited experience with such programs in

the past. Surprisingly, half of the city and consortium
prime sponsors in the sample, as well as half the counties, had no experience with manpower programs, other
than the Public Employment Program (PEP) in fiscal
1974.

Type of Sponsor	Programs Sponsored Before CETA		
	PEP and Others	PEP Only	None
City	3	3	0
County	4	4	1
Consortium	5	4	0
	12	11	1

None of the nine county governments in the sample
studied had much exposure to manpower programs.
Four had operated work experience programs, but four
others had experience only with PEP (although cities
within some of these counties had conducted other
programs).

Even in consortia that include fairly sizable urban
centers, local governments per se often had been mere
bystanders. This was true in Lansing, Kansas City,
Orange County (Cal.), and the Pinellas-St. Petersburg
(Fla.) Consortia, in which manpower programs were
sponsored by schools, the employment service, community-action agencies and other community-based organizations. In the five other consortia in the sample,
local governments had administered manpower programs.
Austin, Cleveland, and Stockton (San Joaquin Consortium)
had established manpower offices before CETA. The
other two (Phoenix-Maricopa and Raleigh) had also operated some programs.

Among the cities studied, governmental experience
had ranged from virtually none in three cases (Long
Beach (Cal.), St. Paul, and Topeka) to heavy responsibility in the others. Gary and Philadelphia had sponsored CEPs as well as work experience programs prior
to CETA. New York City had the most experience,
dating back to the establishment of the Manpower and
Career Development Agency to pull together the many

fragmented antipoverty and manpower programs through-
out the city. [24]/ Supported mainly by city funds, the
agency subcontracted with community-action and other
organizations to set up a network of outreach and manpower centers. The employment service, community-
based organizations, and many other nonprofit agencies
continued to operate programs outside that system.

It is more difficult to generalize about the prior
experience of local governments now under the state
umbrella. In Maine, North Carolina, and Arizona, the
major programs were not run through local governments,
again except for PEP. In Texas, the patterns were more
complex as county governments, community-action agencies, Services, Employment, Redevelopment (SER), a
community-based organization for Spanish-speaking persons, and councils of government were variously involved.

LOCAL GOVERNMENT TAKES OVER

From an administrative viewpoint, the identification
of a single prime sponsor in each area vested with the
authority to bring order from a confused jumble of relationships was critically important. It is too early to
judge whether this will result in a more efficient and
effective program. However, prime sponsors are assuming responsibility for funding and administering
CETA programs in their jurisdictions with varying speed
and in various manners. State, city, county, and consortium prime sponsors have now gone through the critical phase of establishing machinery to handle the central
administrative functions, some of which were formerly
performed by regional offices.

CETA has reduced communication routes to a single
trunk line from the regional Manpower Administration
office to each prime sponsor. Although the number of

24/ In 1973 the Manpower and Career Development
     Agency was merged with the job referral unit of
     the Department of Social Services to establish the
     Department of Employment, which now administers
     CETA.

organizations providing manpower services has not
been necessarily reduced, most of them are now contractors of local sponsors rather than independent
operators (see Chapter 5).

Where the prime sponsor puts CETA in its organizational structure is important for management efficiency,
and reflects the importance attached to that activity.
The establishment of separate government units to
handle CETA and related functions suggests that manpower programs are becoming institutionalized, as
shown below.

Placement of CETA Unit in Local Government Structure

Type of Sponsor	Manpower Department	Office of Chief Official	Existing Department	Reports to Consortium Board
City	2	2	2	-
County	5	2	2	-
Consortium	3	3	1	2
	10	7	5	2

Ten of the 24 city, county, and consortium prime
sponsors in the study either set up a separate manpower
office to handle the planning and administration of CETA,
or merged CETA with an existing manpower agency
(Austin, Cleveland, New York). This form of organization focuses the activity of the staff specifically on the
objectives of the act. Such organization enhances the
importance of the manpower function and establishes it
as part of the basic institutional structure with status
equal to other major departments. The current concern
over rising unemployment and the increased levels of
CETA funding usually gives the manpower administrator
direct access to the chief administrative officer.

Another approach, used by seven of the sponsors,
was to set up the manpower office as a unit in the city
or county executive's office. While this approach takes
advantage of the direct attention of the chief elected or
administrative official, it has less visibility than does a
separate line department.

In five of the cases the manpower function was assigned to a division or unit within one of the established departments, such as the personnel office. Under this arrangement, the organizational distance between manpower and the chief executive is greater, and the head of the manpower office must compete for the attention of a department chief who has other responsibilities.

In seven of the consortia, the manpower unit is responsible to the central city or county in the consortium, yet it may also report to a consortium board or executive committee. In two cases, the administrator's office was established as a separate unit responsible only to a consortium board.

Patterns vary, but the central fact is clear: the administration of manpower programs is being integrated into the local government structure. Manpower is becoming an increasingly visible area of public administration.

ADMINISTRATIVE HEADACHES

Decentralization requires shifting from regional to local and state officials responsibility for fiscal accounting, reporting, contract administration, supervision of contractors' performance, and assessment of results. The survey found that many local administrators are having difficulty in assuming these administrative responsibilities.

There are two basic administrative patterns: some CETA administrators are operating a few programs directly and subcontracting for others; in other areas, the prime sponsor takes a narrower, purely administrative view and all operating activities are subcontracted.

Typically the manpower office is responsible for program supervision but receives support from regular departments of the local government for technical services. There are varying degrees of supervision over program operators. In Topeka for example, the central administrative functions (supervising contracts and monitoring operations) are handled by the manpower planning office, but that office uses other city departments for auxiliary functions. Vouchers are approved by the manpower administrator and paid by the city finance office. Similarly, all subcontracts are cleared through the legal office. The staff of Topeka's subcontractors are paid directly by the city so that they tend to be closely related to the city's administration.

Prime sponsors have had problems in establishing administrative machinery. The complexity of the programs, the need for reconciling diverse interests, pressures from program operators and client groups, and cumbersome procedures call for considerable management skill. These difficulties were aggravated by the deadlines set by the Manpower Administration.

Staff inexperience was the most serious problem mentioned in the survey responses. In the initial task of staffing the central administrative unit, several local sponsors chose administrators with backgrounds in manpower programs. Others recruited former Manpower Area Planning Council planners or local model cities officers. The remaining sponsors appointed persons with backgrounds unrelated to the top jobs.

CETA administrative units range from a staff of two in a relatively small county to over 100 for Title I alone in New York City and as many as 45 in an agency set up for the balance of a state. Staff drawn from former planning groups were familiar with manpower programs but often lacked management skills. Some units were forced to rely on completely new staff who had only the foggiest notion of manpower. Even in cities such as Gary, Austin, New York, Cleveland, and Stockton, which had prior programs, the CETA staff had much to learn in a very short time.

The local CETA administrators must coordinate the interests of planning councils, elected officials, and program operators. In a consortium, the job is even more complex since the interests of all components must be reconciled as well. In one consortium, for example, the manpower unit in the office of the city manager of the central city must deal with two elected groups, a city council and a county board of supervisors, as well as with a consortium board and a manpower planning council.

The balancing of the administrative staffs of consortia so that the interests of all partners are protected is a common expedient. In the example just cited, the CETA administrator is a former county employee, while the three top aides were appointed by the city. Another consortium, consisting of several large cities, performed its balancing act by including a manpower planner from each of the cities. The administrator is obviously subject to multiple political pressures in these situations. Compounding the difficulties of administration are the tensions produced when, for example, a county takes over programs formerly operated by cities within its borders. Discontinuity in policy and administrative direction resulting from the frequent turnover of elected officials pose additional hindrances.

The most extreme example of administrative difficulties occurred in a county without previous experience that tried to assume all operational and administrative functions. After a period of manpower regional office stewardship, the prime sponsor has reverted to a more modest role. Although this example is not typical, the kinds of problems found there--lack of experience, tight deadlines, understaffing, lack of timely technical assistance--are found in other areas to some degree.

In a review of prime sponsors' performance conducted by the Manpower Administration in May 1975, 235 of a total of 402 were judged to be performing satisfactorily, 114 were considered marginal, and 53 were rated as "significant underperformers." Two general kinds of problems were cited frequently: delays in expending allotments and administrative/organizational difficulties. Among the latter were excessive administrative costs, ineffective internal management information systems, poor internal organization, and ineffective use of staff.

The continuing interruption of CETA by requirements stemming from appropriation changes, new legislation, and increased emphasis on public service employment in many cases overwhelmed local sponsors in their efforts to install and administer comprehensive programs under Title I. Despite these problems most prime sponsors studied were able to get Title I under way.

ELECTED OFFICIALS

One of the basic assumptions of decentralization is that elected officials and the community at large would become more concerned with manpower once they were more than only marginally involved. The first survey has found that manpower programs are indeed becoming a significant area of government concern and attention at state and local levels. While day-to-day administration is delegated, elected local officials in most areas have participated in setting up the organizational structure and in making key decisions regarding goals and priorities.

There are, of course, differences in the degree to which elected officials exercise administrative control, depending on the structure of local government. In the council-manager form of government, powers are delegated to administrative officials. In large cities and counties where the elected officials are also the chief executives, responsibility for supervision and administration is delegated to aides or department heads. Even in such cases, there is apparently greater awareness on the part of elected officials than there was before CETA.

The impact of CETA on elected officials is most strikingly seen in county governments newly exposed to manpower programs. In these situations elected officials tend to maintain close contact with manpower officials and to keep abreast of administrative developments. The reason for this heightened interest is not hard to find-- the shift of authority and with it the control of a considerable amount of funds and number of jobs. One county received CETA allocations of some $9 million in fiscal 1975, compared with a total county budget of $66 million. In another county, CETA funds account for $3 million of a $10.5 million county budget.

In consortia too, elected officials are more active through participation on consortium boards. The Lansing consortium is a good example. Previously, elected officials (other than the mayor of Lansing) had little control over manpower activities. Now 12 elected officials, representing the city of Lansing and three counties, are on the board. Although the actual administration is carried out by the staff, board members participate in setting goals and priorities and approving criteria and plans for evaluation. They have been particularly interested in an equitable method of allotting resources and selecting program operators.

The concern of elected officials in cities is greater than ever, although in the larger cities mayors necessarily rely on department heads. CETA is regarded as a positive and visible instrument for dealing with critical unemployment problems even in cities that have established manpower programs.

Title VI, which makes available federally funded public service jobs, significantly increased the interest and involvement of elected officials in manpower programs. Title II and Title VI funds are channeled to smaller units of government within counties, consortia, and the balance of states, and this also tends to broaden the political support for manpower programs. As one prime sponsor said, "Jobs is votes, and votes is jobs."

The aim of decentralization is to make manpower programs more responsive to local needs through the local political process. The authority of local elected officials over manpower programs makes them susceptible to pressures from politically potent program operators and client groups with interests to advance. New channels of communication, formal and informal, are now open to individuals and groups. Local officials are probably more accessible than federal officials in the selection of target groups and service deliverers. There have been cases reported where elected officials have not accepted recommendations of the planning council as a result of local pressure. In one consortium, for instance, a community-based organization won a major operating role after a delegation of ministers visited the mayor. In another area, the consortium board awarded a manpower center contract to a county government rather than to a combination of community-based organizations recommended by the planning council.

Some elected officials are content to allow decisions to be made by the planning council and staff, but in most cases, as the elected officials become more conscious of their authority and responsibility, manpower programs

are being brought increasingly into the political process.
In some cases, political officials are interested in decisions regarding deliverers of manpower services, in
other areas the concern is with the clientele to be served.
The tendency has been to broaden the client base, which
apparently reflects their perception of the desires of the
electorate. It is difficult to determine whether such
decisions are responsive to the needs of the community
as a whole or to the segment of the community that is at
a disadvantage.

While the survey did not focus on this question,
there are indications of political clearance in the appointment of CETA administrators and staff, most of whom
are not under merit systems. There have also been
allegations of patronage in selection of participants. In
one case, the Manpower Administration has transferred
responsibility for selection of Title II and Title VI participants from the prime sponsor to the state-run employment service. However, there is no evidence that such
practices have been widespread.

THE STATE'S ROLE

One of the issues considered in framing the CETA
legislation was the role of state government. In the interplay of forces that led to enactment of CETA, state governments were bypassed as funding conduits in favor of
a stronger and more direct role for city and county governments. However, the states were given responsibility
for manpower programs in balance-of-state areas (areas
not under the jurisdiction of other prime sponsors). The
state was also given a general statewide planning, coordinating, and monitoring function through the SMSC. In
effect, states were assigned part of the former regional
office monitoring function but without sufficient authority
to carry out the part effectively.

In comparing the manpower functions of the state
before and after CETA, a distinction must be made between the direct role of the governor and the legislatively
mandated responsibilities of the traditional state manpower agencies. Before CETA, the governors' offices

were involved in planning but had little direct role in
administering manpower programs. State employment
security and education agencies administered MDTA
training programs with little supervision or control by
the governor. When these old-line state agencies lost
the franchise they had held under MDTA, their authority
over local manpower programs diminished considerably.
The governor's direct responsibility has enlarged. For
the first time, manpower funds for the balance of states
are funneled through the governor's office.

States discharge their dual responsibilities--
administering balance-of-state programs and the SMSC--
in two ways. In three of the four states in the sample
(Arizona, North Carolina, Maine), both functions are
assigned to a single state agency; in Texas functions
were divided (see Chapter 3, page 63).

Before CETA, State Manpower Planning Councils
reviewed local plans and forwarded them to Manpower
Administration regional offices. In some states, assistance to local AMPBs was provided by the state planning
office (see page 50). Under CETA, the SMSC reviews
all local plans, but, at least during the first year, this
review was described as perfunctory. In several states,
SMSCs were just being formed or were relatively inactive
at the time that plans were drawn up. State governments
had almost no influence on the local prime sponsor programs through the formal planning process, perhaps
even less than before CETA.

SMSCs are also responsible for coordinating efforts
to meet the overall manpower needs of the state, but
interviews at the state and local level indicated that this
kind of activity was not even on the horizon when this
survey was made. Indeed most prime sponsors have
been so absorbed in the urgent tasks of management and
program development that they have given little thought
to coordination with other areas. Some state councils
are conscious of their assigned role in monitoring local
programs, but the first survey did not reveal any significant activity. The nearest that the states have come
toward discharging their monitoring function are the
decisions of some to use part of the manpower services
fund to develop data that could help local sponsors in
self-appraisal.

Manpower Services Fund

CETA requires that 4 percent of Title I funds be distributed to the states to provide statewide services, assist rural programs, furnish labor market information and technical assistance, and to fund model programs.

A survey of 33 states by the U. S. Governor's Conference showed that states plan to use 40 percent of the money for such statewide services as apprenticeship, affirmative action programs, and computerized job placement, and 36 percent on special prototype programs for such groups as offenders and handicapped persons.[25]

Although some prime sponsors in the sample are represented on SMSCs, most reported they were not consulted on how the 4 percent fund was to be used. Six indicated that data systems were to be supported by the state from this fund. Other areas reported that the state planned to use the fund for model programs and for technical assistance. The consensus was that the 4 percent fund had no significant effect on local prime sponsor programs.

CETA also provides that 5 percent of Title I funds be allocated to governors for supplemental vocational education services. The supplemental vocational education fund that was allotted to local sponsors was more immediately and directly useful than the manpower services fund, but prime sponsors did not find it critical to their operations.

On the whole, the role of state governments has not been significant under CETA except in the balance-of-state programs. The influence and control conferred on the states by CETA are insufficient to accomplish the coordination among prime sponsors mandated by the act. Neither the 4 percent services fund, the 5 percent vocational education fund, nor the SMSC provide the leverage necessary for any significant impact upon local programs.

Balance-of-State Programs

The administration of balance-of-state (BOS) programs is handled variously. In one state it is completely

[25] Reported in the Manpower Administration's Interchange 1(7):5, 1974.

centralized; other states are in the process of shifting much of the responsibility to substate government units.

The trend toward decentralization is manifested in three of the four states surveyed. Texas has delegated authority to 15 councils of government and to two community-action agencies under a regional form of administration; Arizona has a similar arrangement. Four councils of government, the Navajo Nation, and the Indian Development District are subgrantees of the state. Each council allocates resources to counties and cities within its domain and the program operators now deal with the councils. Program administration in North Carolina was initially handled directly by the state, but an attempt is being made to establish Lead Regional Organizations (similar to Councils of Government) as administrative units. In Maine, where an attempt was made to operate the entire program at the state level, two of the larger counties (Penobscot and Cumberland, with populations of over 100,000) have broken away and are now prime sponsors.26/

Prior to CETA there were few multi-county manpower programs in rural sections of balance-of-state areas except in the instances where employment service offices, school systems, and community-action agencies operated across county lines. This is still basically true under CETA. However, CETA has stimulated area cooperation by investing regional planning organizations with a substantive administration role, thereby strengthening regional organizations and developing a new administrative structure between county and state governments that could well have implications for other governmental functions. Such intergovernmental arrangements will require a great deal of technical assistance and supervision if they are to assume a more important role in manpower programs.

26/ Those counties were not designated as prime sponsors initially because at that time the county governments in Maine were not judged to be fully functioning government units.

FORMING CONSORTIA

In an effort to accomplish by voluntary agreement what it was unwilling to mandate, CETA authorized the use of up to 5 percent of Title I funds as incentives to areas that form consortia--jurisdictions eligible to be prime sponsors in their own right and surrounding smaller counties or cities.[27/] The results exceeded expectations. It had been thought that consortia would be a difficult and unstable form of local organization because of interjurisdictional rivalries. However, 135 have been established in fiscal 1975, comprising one-third of the 402 prime sponsors.[28/]

The decisive factors in the formation of consortia were mutual trust based on previous successful joint efforts and the ability to agree on the distribution of authority and resources. In some cases the central cities were thought to have advantages that would benefit the surrounding areas: competence in handling manpower programs, experienced planning staff, and service deliverers operating across jurisdictional lines. Other considerations were greater opportunities for job development based on a broader labor market, and economies of scale. In several cases the desire to participate in manpower programs through the anonymity of a consortium, thereby avoiding the political hazards of direct responsibility, played a part in the decision. Small areas, faced with the option of becoming part of the balance-of-state program or of joining a nearby consortium, often chose the latter.

Contrary to expectation, the financial incentive offered for forming consortia was apparently not a decisive factor in most cases. Six of the consortia in the sample

27/ Five percent of the Title I funds, distributed among sponsors eligible for incentives, amounted to 10 percent for each.

28/ A total of 497 jurisdictions of 100,000 or more were potentially eligible to become prime sponsors. Of these 224 (45 percent) combined to form consortia. Sixty-four percent of cities and 40 percent of counties of 100,000 or more were in consortia in fiscal 1975.

mentioned incentives as having a bearing on forming a consortium, but only one considered it very important.

Consortia were not organized without hard bargaining and compromises among the jurisdictions. Some negotiations revolved around the allocation of funds. In the Austin and Phoenix consortia the counties received more than their proportional shares as an added inducement to join the consortium. In other areas there were political trade-offs. Those commonly related to the designation of the central governmental unit, selection of administrator and staff, representation of the consortium board, selection of the advisory council chairmen, and designation of service deliverers to assure services to all geographic components. In one case an elaborate formula was used for suballocation of funds, based on the number of unemployed heads of households in each jurisdiction, school dropouts, and economically disadvantaged; in another a "fair share" formula was used, based on each city's share of the poverty population.

There were also legal and administrative problems to be worked out. Typically a form of joint powers agreement was drawn up, assigning overall responsibility to a consortium board or executive committee made up of delegates of each of the areas and assigning administrative responsibility to a lead city or county.

Despite interjurisdictional problems, consortia appear to be stable; relatively few changes are taking place in their number or composition. The latest count numbers 137 consortia in fiscal 1976, about the same number as the year before. Of the nine consortia in the sample, only one has had a serious split because of irreconcilable city-county conflicts. Wake County has left the Raleigh consortium to apply for prime sponsorship in a dispute between county and city officials over the nature of the consortium including the role of a community-action agency. On the other hand, the balance of Shawnee County (population 30,000) joined Topeka to form an additional consortium. This arrangement will give county residents access to city manpower services instead of dependence on the state.

Each of the 15 cities and counties in the sample had considered participating in a consortium and decided against it.   Resistance was based mainly on the differences between the population in the inner cities and the suburbs, desire for sole administrative control by local government units, and fear of dominance by central cities.   Six of the 15 are suburban or satellite communities, which decided to set up independent programs to concentrate on serving their own constituents.   CETA gave them the opportunity to establish or reinforce institutions in their own communities responsive to what they believe to be their unique needs.   To a lesser extent, political rivalries among jurisdictions also affected their decisions to stand alone.   In those cases in which the prime sponsor was a central city or county, the major reason for not forming a consortium was the opposite side of the coin. Gary, for example, preferred to maintain programs for its own constituents.

THE REGIONAL OFFICE ROLE

The relationship between the regional offices of the Manpower Administration and local sponsors is one measure of decentralization.   It was assumed that under CETA regional offices would no longer control but would have oversight responsibilities for programs and would interpret regulations and provide technical assistance. The findings of the study suggest that this change has not yet been completely achieved, although there are significant variations among areas.   In the past, the regional offices had an intermediate role in allocating funds and making tactical decisions.   National categorical programs with their specific guidelines were the basis for selecting groups to be served and service deliverers. Except for resources that were distributed by formula, grants and funding decisions were made by the regional or national office.   In addition, the regional office interpreted guidelines to local project operators, monitored programs, and supervised local contracts.   However, the presence of regional office personnel and the manner in which federal officials carried out their responsibilities prior to CETA varied among regions and even among staff within the same region.

During the first year of CETA, despite the transfer of program control to prime sponsors (or perhaps because of it), regional presence was intensive. Guidelines and regulations are detailed and complicated, and since many prime sponsors were unfamiliar with administrative procedures and program operations, demands on the regional offices were heavy.

Because of unequal capabilities among prime sponsors and differences in the operating style of regional office personnel, the degree of federal involvement and influence in local affairs varied from domination to a hands-off posture. Regional office field representatives worked out a modus vivendi with the prime sponsors varying with the local situation. Some were content to respond to problems brought to their attention. Others actively participated in decisions on the substance of programs and administration, including such activities as attending council meetings, policing statistical and financial reports, and assisting in organizing management information systems.

There was a general feeling of uncertainty as to appropriate activities of regional office staff, which reflected the gray area between the local autonomy of prime sponsors and the oversight responsibilities of federal authorities. Disagreement between prime sponsors and federal representatives was common. In one case the federal representative viewed his responsibilities comprehensively, touching on all aspects of program development, but the CETA administrator perceived the federal representative's role as limited to interpretation of regulations. Cases were reported in which the regional office exerted strong influence on such matters as specifying groups to be served and shaping the delivery system. In other situations, the regional office role was supportive and advisory. On the whole, the federal pressure for a comprehensive manpower design and the elimination of duplication was clearly evident in discussions, comments, advice, and correspondence.

One regional office role that was not questioned was the review of Title I plans. These plans are the key to the federal purse. In some cases federal representatives were in on the planning process early so that Title I plans received prompt approval. In others, plans were returned several times because of deficiencies. In one instance, regional office comments dealt with the inadequacies of the intake system, integration of programs, designation of groups in need, and failure to include training in English as a second language. In another case, shortcomings were noted in staffing, organization, the administrative plan, client and fiscal records and information systems, and procedures for selecting deliverers of services. But most observations were reported to be technical rather than substantive, dealing with such matters as need for more justification or supporting data.

As the program moved toward implementation, regional office supervision increased. Regional office representatives interviewed early in 1975 expressed increasing concern over delays in filling Title I and Title II openings in the face of rising unemployment. This concern was reflected in criticisms of those CETA administrators who had not been able to carry out programs as rapidly as the Manpower Administration had stipulated or as set forth in plans.

In two prime sponsor areas in the sample, it was necessary for the regional office to intervene in program administration. In one, the federal representative was obliged to supervise closely the recruiting of staff, to develop administrative procedures, to arrange for technical assistance and training, and to assist in day-to-day operations. The CETA operation in that county became a joint venture. In another situation the federal representative has been installed in the CETA central administrative and planning office as on-site monitor, largely because of allegations of political influence.

Prime sponsors' reactions to regional offices ranged from expressions of appreciation for assistance to criticism of excessive demands and red tape. While CETA has reduced federal reporting requirements, it has shifted the burden of assembling statistical data from regional offices to prime sponsors. This has been difficult for CETA administrators and has become a source of friction with regional offices. One CETA administrator felt that the excessive regulations and detailed records threatened the decentralization process. The clash in role definition was expressed by prime sponsors in various ways. Some felt that the regional office was unwilling to adjust to the CETA concept of local autonomy; one accused the regional office of being bound by a "bureaucratic set" that precluded innovations. Another felt that the regional office was reluctant to relinquish direct control over program operators.

This transition period is not the best time to ascertain whether the shift of responsibilities from regional offices to prime sponsors has simplified management or made it more complex. The new administrative layer--the prime sponsor--that CETA has introduced between the federal government and the program operator could make for tighter monitoring and evaluation of program operations by sponsors, who are closer to the scene than regional offices. However, the lack of management information and evaluation criteria has made it difficult to carry out this responsibility so far. As roles are stabilized and both regional offices and prime sponsors become accustomed to their new responsibilities, the administrative processes may work more smoothly.

SUMMARY

The first year under CETA has posed administrative challenges to prime sponsors as they took over responsibility for the management of programs.

- CETA has brought manpower programs under the administration of local governments, some of which had minimal experience with such programs.
- Manpower is becoming institutionalized as a significant area of public administration. In most cases separate offices have been set up--often with departmental status--to operate manpower programs.
- Establishing the administrative machinery has entailed difficulties in staffing and coordination. The frequent interruptions caused by new legislation and plan modifications resulting from changes in the labor market have added to the turmoil.

- Manpower programs are being brought closer to the local political process as elected officials become more involved in administration. Political influences are affecting program decisions to a greater degree than before as officials respond to local pressures.

- The role of state governments under CETA is less clearly defined than that of local governments. Aside from administration of balance-of-state programs, the states seem at the outset to have little effect in the coordination or monitoring of local programs. The 4 percent manpower services fund and the 5 percent supplemental vocational education fund have done little to give states leverage. Three of the four states in the sample are decentralizing administration of balance-of-state programs to regional organizations such as councils of government, which have little experience in administration of manpower programs.

- CETA has encouraged interjurisdictional arrangements; one-third of all prime sponsors are consortia. The major reason for forming consortia has been successful experience in joint planning or operation of programs. Areas that did not form consortia preferred to manage their own programs independent of jurisdictions, which they perceived as having different populations and manpower problems. Despite problems of reconciling diverse interests, eight of the nine consortia sampled have continued into the second year.

- The role of regional offices relative to prime sponsors is a key to decentralization. Interpretation of role varies as do the style of federal officials in carrying out responsibilities, and some feeling exists on the part of local sponsors that regional office interference is excessive. On the whole prime sponsors have assumed their new responsibilities, but there were signs of growing regional office involvement as unemployment rose.

5

The Delivery System

The Comprehensive Employment and Training Act (CETA) frees the manpower system from the rigidities imposed by separate funding sources, regulations, reporting systems, and institutional frameworks that isolated 17 separate programs from one another. CETA permits the prime sponsor to restructure or maintain the combinations of programs and institutions through which manpower services are delivered: assessment, orientation, training, placement, counselling, and followup. Providing a range of services in a comprehensive system while encouraging efficiency and eliminating overlap is a major objective of manpower reform.

Chapter 5 describes changes in the manpower delivery system resulting from the shift of control from federal to local authorities. It observes the effect of prime sponsor hegemony over local program operators and the changes in the role of institutions that traditionally have provided manpower services. Particular attention is directed to the extent to which programs are decategorized by integrating and coordinating manpower activities.

Prior to CETA the local employment service and vocational education agencies played the leading role in providing skill training. In a single community, however, there often were additional training or

work-experience programs operated variously by
community-based organizations, schools, or other
agencies.   No consistent pattern was discernible; it
was not uncommon to have several delivery systems
with seemingly similar objectives but little coordination
except for token cooperation through a weak planning
committee.

The agencies delivering manpower services often
competed for limited resources, for program participants, and for jobs or training slots to serve their
clients.   In large jurisdictions, competition and duplication were apparent; in smaller areas those problems
were less prevalent.

Prior to CETA the delivery system often lacked
flexibility.   Typically, each separate program offered a
limited range of services and training options.   Except
for concentrated employment programs (CEPs), most
programs had focused on specific activities.   A comprehensive system, it was felt, would be able to offer a
wider range of services that would permit the tailoring
of an individual program according to a client's needs.

Finally, it was felt that the local manpower system
would be more productive if, unlike the pre-CETA situation, there were no presumptive deliverers of manpower
services.   The established manpower agencies must now
compete for service contracts and convince the prime
sponsor that they are the best buy in terms of performance
and costs.   However prime sponsors must give consideration to programs "of demonstrated effectiveness" and
use existing services ". . . to the extent deemed
appropriate."

The spectrum of programs before CETA has been
alluded to; a typical county might look something like
Stanislaus County (Cal.):

Sponsoring Agengy	Program[29]/
Stanislaus County (with community action agency)	NYC out-of-school Operation Mainstream
Stanislaus County	Public Employment Program

29/ See Appendix A for a list of pre-CETA programs
     and acronyms.

Sponsoring Agency	Program
Modesto city schools	NYC in-school
	Summer youth
Employment service and Modesto Junior College	MDTA skill training
Employment service	MDTA individual referral
	MDTA on-the-job training
	Public Service Careers
National Alliance of Businessmen (and employment service)	Job Opportunities in the Business Sector

In cities it was not uncommon to find a larger number of Department of Labor funded programs, as well as components of the Work Incentive Program and projects with manpower components sponsored by other agencies, such as the Department of Housing and Urban Development, the Department of Justice, and the Office of Economic Opportunity.[30/]

In areas that became consortia the situation was more complex because of the combination of cities and counties with different programs. The main focus of activity was in the central city, but often the city programs overlapped jurisdictional boundaries, as in the Raleigh Consortium:

City/County	Sponsoring Agency	Program
Raleigh/Wake	City of Raleigh	Public Employment Program
		Summer youth
	Employment service and county technical institute	MDTA skill training
	Employment Service	MDTA JOPS
	Wake Opportunities	Public Service Careers

[30/] Now Community Services Agency.

City/County	Sponsoring Agency	Program
Raleigh/Wake	Wake Opportunities	NYC in-school NYC out-of-school Summer youth
Wake County	Wake County	Public Employment Program
Lee County	Employment service and county technical institute	MDTA skill training
	Employment service	MDTA JOPS NYC in-school Summer youth
	State of North Carolina	Public Employment Program
Johnston County Chatham County	Employment service and county technical institute	MDTA skill training
	Employment service	MDTA JOPS
	Board of education	NYC in-school Summer Youth
	State of North Carolina	Public Employment Program

Areas that are now in the balance of state had not been under central administration before CETA so that there too the pattern of delivery varied considerably. In North Carolina, for example, MDTA programs were operated in various local areas by the employment service in cooperation with the community college system. In addition, the employment service administered MDTA on-the-job training (JOPs) and in one case a rural CEP. Work experience programs (Neighborhood Youth Corps and Operation Mainstream) were conducted by community-action agencies and by school boards.

THE TRANSITION

Local governments trying to set up a program delivery system under CETA were faced with an array of programs already in place. Manpower Administration instructions permitted several arrangements for dealing with current programs. MDTA programs were allowed to continue under their sponsors until scheduled termination dates but not later than December 1974. Categorical programs under EOA could either continue until termination or be taken over immediately by the prime sponsor. In most cases sponsors chose the former course so that for the first six months, dual systems operated in many areas. Upon termination of contracts prime sponsors had the option of 1) subcontracting with existing project operators to continue their activities; 2) modifying the projects to correspond with the sponsor's plan; 3) dropping the program altogether; 4) transferring all or part of it to another contractor; or 5) absorbing the activities of the program into the prime sponsor's own operation. In cases where existing programs were to be discontinued or changed, prime sponsors were urged to mitigate hardship for trainees by allowing them to complete their courses.

As the changeover took place there was inevitably a considerable amount of dislocation among agencies and personnel operating manpower programs. Some expertise in managing programs was lost, some equipment and facilities for training wasted, and valuable contacts with potential employers disrupted. Prime sponsors were confronted with the simultaneous tasks of planning for CETA and coping with the immediate problems of program operation. The task was not easy; before they had gotten their feet wet they were faced with a series of unexpected developments.

The Emergency Employment Act (EEA), which was to have expired in June 1974, was continued through March 1975 by an authorization of $250 million. Prime sponsors had to make arrangements quickly to extend the termination dates of public service employees working under EEA or hire new ones. At the same time, $397 million was made available for the 1974 summer youth programs. Prime sponsors had either to set up their own machinery or, on very short notice, to find organizations to run that program during the summer of 1974.

Simultaneously, it was necessary to implement Title II of CETA, which opened up transitional public service jobs for unemployed and underemployed persons living in areas of substantial unemployment (rates of 6.5 percent or more for three consecutive months).   This title had its own set of rules and regulations, including a "pass through" provision requiring prime sponsors to suballocate funds to cities or counties of 50,000 or more. Congress appropriated $370 million for Title II late in fiscal 1974 and $400 million in the fall of fiscal 1975.

By that time the economic climate had changed radically and recession was on the horizon.   The national unemployment rate shot up from 4.5 percent in December 1973 when CETA was passed, to over 7 percent a year later, and worse was yet to come.   The Emergency Jobs and Unemployment Assistance Act of 1974 (EJUAA) was speeded through Congress and signed by the President. The act established a new Title VI authorizing $2.5 billion for public service jobs in fiscal 1975.   Congress appropriated $1 billion of this amount. [31]/ The enactment of EJUAA added to CETA a large new categorical program with another set of regulations and requirements.

It is little wonder that prime sponsors faltered in their efforts to assume responsibility for establishing a new system for delivery of manpower services.   Early plans for Title I had to be adjusted to the realities of a changed labor market.   Its implementation was moved to the back burner and efforts to deal with spiraling unemployment through Title II and Title VI took priority.   The introduction of Title VI diverted the attention of manpower officials from their comprehensive manpower programs (Title I) before they were fully established.   Moreover, prime sponsors found themselves in the fiscal 1976 planning cycle before they were organized for fiscal 1975.

CHANGING INSTITUTIONS

Under these circumstances sponsors had limited opportunity during the first year to make substantial changes in the institutional framework for program

31/ $125 million of the $1 billion went to the Department of Commerce for job creation projects.

operations. The study finds that although there was generally a continuity of program operators and program content, significant changes are occurring in many areas. The structure that emerges is a coalition of existing programs under local government auspices. Most prime sponsors continued contracts with existing program operators for training, work experience, and service activities, but modifications were made to achieve better coordination.

Of the 254 pre-CETA programs identified in the sample areas, 67 percent were renewed or continued by the prime sponsor (56 percent with no change and 11 percent with change).[32] This includes programs operated by prime sponsors before CETA (mainly public employment) and continued in the same manner after its enactment. Conversely, one-third of the pre-existing pro-programs have either been discontinued (10 percent) or have changed hands (23 percent).[33]

Programs are most stable in consortia, in which there has generally been more prior experience in manpower planning and administration. Changes are also more difficult to arrange in a multijurisdictional setting. In Raleigh, Austin, and Phoenix, for example, the outlying counties insisted on maintaining the programs operating in their areas. Cities tended to continue existing programs more than counties. Programs most likely to be dropped were Public Service Careers and Job Opportunities in the Business Sector (JOBS).

32/ In 23 areas, 254 pre-CETA programs were identified (New York and balance-of-state programs omitted). A "program" refers to a categorical program (such as MDTA institutional, JOP, PSC, and NYC in-school) operated by one sponsor or contractor. Only first-tier contractors were counted; thus a CEP program with a number of subcontractors was counted as one program.

33/ Among discontinued programs were a number of summer youth projects which may have been reinstated when the fiscal 1975 summer youth appropriation was approved.

Table 15. Disposition of Pre-CETA Manpower Programs Under CETA, by Type of Local Sponsor

Type of Sponsor	Programs Be-fore CETA	All Pro-grams	Discon-tinued	Subcontracted		Transferred To	
				With Change	With-out Change	Prime Spon-sor	Other Oper-ator
City[a]/	58	100	16	10	55	10	9
County	76	100	11	8	38	35	8
Consor-tium	120	100	6	13	68	9	3
ALL SPON-SORS	254	100	10	11	56	17	6

a/ New York omitted.
(Details may not add to totals due to rounding.)

Prime Sponsors as Program Operators

        The extent to which prime sponsors themselves have decided to operate manpower programs is one of the more significant developments under CETA. Prior to CETA, 15 percent of the local programs were operated directly by the government unit that became a prime sponsor or, in the case of a consortium, that administers programs for for the consortium. Under CETA, the proportion of programs active prior to CETA being operated by the sponsor has risen to 33 percent.
        The most frequent changes were the transfer of some responsibilities from the employment service or community-action agency to prime sponsors. Usually the change was in the scope of activities. In Lorain County (Oh.), for example, the employment service operated institutional and on-the-job training programs before CETA. Under CETA, the prime sponsor has taken over responsibility for operating these programs, but the employment service still provides for intake,

Table 16. Selected Manpower Programs Operated by Local Sample Prime Sponsor Before CETA and Under CETA

Selected Pre-CETA Program Category	Number in Local Sample Areas[a]/	Operated by Prime Sponsor	
		Before CETA	Under CETA[b]/
MDTA institutional	40	0	8
MDTA JOPS	18	0	7
JOBS	16	0	4
NYC in-school	30	2	7
NYC out-of-school	24	4	10
Summer youth	25	1	5
Operation Mainstream	15	3	7
CEP	4	4	4

a/ New York omitted.
b/ Equivalent to pre-CETA categorical program.

assessment and testing, job placement, and handling of training allowances. Thus the transfer of program responsibility does not necessarily eliminate the former program operator from all activities. In Union County, (N. J.), a community-action agency operated NYC programs. Under CETA these programs are run by the county through manpower centers. The community-action agency has lost its operating role, but has contracted to locate two staff members in a county-run manpower center.

Decisions to change or retain deliverers of service had to be made very quickly, and no sound, objective basis for such decisions existed. Prospective operators submitted proposals but generally competitive bids were not used during the first year. There was room for judgment, local pressures, and political maneuvering. Only a few areas used some type of formal performance evaluation to choose among bidders. Elsewhere decisions were based on informal appraisal of past performance, availability of facilities, lack of alternatives, cost, and the desire of some prime sponsors to build their own programs.

One county, for example, was reluctant to contract with the employment service because it considered its performance to be only minimally adequate. In the absence of an objective basis for excluding the employment service and with insufficient time to assume the necessary activities, the county acceded to regional office pressure and contracted with the employment service.

For the most part prime sponsors took one of two approaches. Some assumed as much control as practicable; others preferred to continue with the existing establishments at least during the first year. Where prime sponsors received substantial increases in allocations over 1974 funds, decisions were easier to reach. Other sponsors had difficult choices to make in allocating reduced resources. In one area a point system was used to evaluate prospective manpower delivery systems, giving heavy weight to past experience.

COORDINATING MANPOWER SERVICES

Prior to CETA there was little coordination among local manpower programs except in cities where CEPs or other comprehensive programs existed. Charges of duplication were made repeatedly.

In highly populated areas with a number of categorical programs there was overlap in administration and in types of training offered by competing programs. For example, adult basic education was offered in the public schools under MDTA, but community-based organizations set up similar courses for their clients. The employment service and community-based organizations conducted the same kind of intake and assessment activities. Duplication was particularly serious with respect to job development and placement as a number of programs vied for employers' job openings.

In smaller localities there was less confusion and competition. Most programs were aimed at distinct population or age groups or specific geographic areas, using different approaches and techniques. NYC and summer youth programs, for example, were for school age youth, and Operation Mainstream enrolled older workers.

Some coordinated programs did exist before CETA. In Phoenix, for example, a CEP was sponsored by the city and operated on its behalf by a community-action agency in the neighborhoods of greatest need. The employment service, the Opportunities Industrialization Center (OIC), and Services, Employment, Redevelopment (SER) subcontracted with the community-action agency for some manpower services, and the schools were tied in for classroom training.

There was more extensive coordination of pre-CETA programs in the Cleveland, Austin, and Stockton (San Joaquin) areas and to some extent in New York City. In Austin, the city had incorporated the community-action agency as a division of the city government to operate th NYC Public Service Careers (PSC), and Mainstream programs. It also subcontracted with another community-action agency to run work-experience programs in 10 surrounding rural counties. In Stockton a number of programs run independently by the employment service, vocational education, and community-based organizations were brought together under an innovative agreement in fiscal 1974 in a move anticipating manpower revenue sharing. The city became the prime sponsor and subcontracted programs back to their previous operators.

Thus there was some movement toward integration of programs and services before CETA. One of the significant accomplishments during the first year under CETA has been a reinforcement of this trend. Most of the prime sponsors in the sample have consolidated at least some overlapping services. This stemmed in part from experience under CEP programs and in part from Manpower Administration stress on comprehensive delivery models.

Delivery Models

Three types of delivery systems were identified in the sample: independent, mixed, and comprehensive.

Each prime sponsor is free to design its own delivery
system, but the historical development of manpower
strategies clearly encourages a comprehensive design.
The Manpower Administration's technical assistance
guide offers several alternatives, but again the stress
is on the comprehensive model.

Of the 28 prime sponsors studied, 13 have maintained an independent delivery system. These sponsors
chose to continue existing programs with minor modifications rather than merging them into an overall design.
Each program independently conducts its activities. In
Topeka and in Chester County (Pa.), for example, the
first consideration of the prime sponsors was to continue
existing programs with only minimal changes.

The state sponsors and several of the consortia fall
into the independent category. They considered comprehensive delivery systems impractical in view of the distances involved and attendant transportation problems.
Areas with independent systems are more likely than
others to add new programs in response to local pressures. In such areas, CETA may result in a more fragmented situation than before.

A second group of sponsors (11) have a mixed delivery system. Some programs and services are consolidated while others operate independently. In those cases
an attempt is made to combine services either by setting
up central intake facilities or by modifying contracts to
provide functional specialization. In Union County, for
example, the organizational framework planned is a
compromise between the pre-existing organization and a
comprehensive system. When the county decided to set
up manpower centers, experienced staff of Plainfield's
manpower office, a community-action agency, and the
employment service were contracted to run centers at
the eastern and western ends of the county. In addition,
the county has separate arrangements with the OIC, the
Urban League, and a private training firm to carry out
other activities and programs.

The Austin consortium is an interesting example of
a mixed situation. Essentially there had been four independent service delivery agencies: the city itself, the
employment service, SER, and a community-action

agency that served outlying areas. Under CETA, a centralized, one-stop manpower center was set up in Austin
by the prime sponsor. SER was eliminated, the employment service does placement and job development for
the manpower center, and the community-action agency
has continued to operate programs in the surrounding
counties.

Before CETA, the New York City Department of
Employment had established a network of 11 regional
manpower training centers and 26 neighborhood centers
in community corporations. The department also subcontracted for components of training and supportive
services with the board of education, City University of
New York, the OIC, and the vocational rehabilitation
agency, among others. The employment service operated a second system, which arranged institutional
training through public and private agencies and conducted an on-the-job training program. A third system used
community-based organizations outside both the city and
the employment service network. Under CETA, the city
has absorbed manpower activities formerly performed
by the employment service, and has set up closer coordination of community-based organizations without completely integrating them.

The Human Resources Economic Development agency
in Cleveland was similar to the earlier New York setup.
Prior to CETA, it operated the CEP, NYC out-of-school,
and PEP programs. It has now taken over almost all of
the manpower services formerly handled by the employment service for MDTA programs. However, the OIC
and the Urban League continue to provide a range of services independently.

Four of 28 prime sponsors in the sample have come
very close to establishing comprehensive systems although complete integration has not been achieved even
in these cases. Under the comprehensive model, services are combined, usually in one or more manpower
centers, but operations, such as classroom training or
work experience, may be subcontracted to other institutions. The pattern among the four comprehensive systems varies, depending largely on relationships between
the prime sponsor and the existing manpower institutions.

Ramsey County (Minn.), which started from scratch,
opted to use the facilities of the employment service to
handle its CETA program. A client entering an employment service office may be referred to a regular employment service counselor or to a manpower counselor,
depending on the client's need to prepare for a job.
(Ramsey County is a high-income suburb of St. Paul
with relatively few economically disadvantaged or
minority group persons.)

In St. Paul itself, where several agencies were
active before CETA, the prime sponsor established a
central facility, bringing components of a number of
public and private nonprofit agencies (Jewish Vocational
Service, Urban League, National Alliance of Businessmen,
the public school district, and the employment service)
under one roof for one-stop service aimed at meeting
individual needs. The Jewish Vocational Service was
selected to manage the center and the role of the employment service was sharply reduced. A few activities
are conducted outside the center. The city has a contract
with the school district for youth career development and
work experience activities and the Urban League continues to manage its own on-the-job training project.

In mid-1975 the San Joaquin consortium set up a
central facility in Stockton close to the population to be
served to advance the coordination of service begun before CETA. This plan would replace the earlier system
in which each program operator maintained its own
facilities, most of which were concentrated in downtown
Stockton within a mile of each other.

In the San Joaquin consortium and in Ramsey County,
the local governments emerge as the principal operator,
unlike St. Paul, where a private nonprofit agency is in
charge, or Long Beach (Cal.), where a community-
action agency has the lead role.

Plans for establishing a comprehensive model do
not always materialize. The difficulties in reorganizing
manpower operations were not fully appreciated, particularly if resistance from entrenched organizations has
been encountered. Calhoun County (Mich.) planned a
comprehensive model that turned out to be an impossible
dream. Under CETA, work experience and training

formerly conducted by the community-action agency and
the employment service were to be performed by the
county through its own office and by outstationed staff.
Lack of experience, administrative problems, and opposition from previous program operators have hampered
the county's implementation of its plan.

In sum, making radical change in organizational'
relationships is very difficult to achieve smoothly. The
ability of threatened bureaucracies to survive, inexperience, and political practicalities have made such change
almost unattainable for the short run.

Changes in the relationships between the prime
sponsor and the institutions that had previously operated
the various manpower programs have been most traumatic.
The following sections describe the effect of CETA on
some of the major deliverers of manpower services.

THE EMPLOYMENT SERVICE

The federal-state employment service with its 40-
year history has a unique place among manpower institutions. It is difficult to generalize about a system of
50 semi-autonomous agencies, a network of over 2,400
offices and some 40,000 employees. Some associate its
longevity with an encrusted bureaucracy unable to respond
to new needs, especially those of the disadvantaged.
Others see the employment service as the repository of
experience in most aspects of manpower activities:
bringing employers and job seekers together, counseling job applicants, and developing labor market
information.

Despite efforts during the 1960s to make the Employment Service more responsive to the manpower needs
of those at a disadvantage in the job market, many of
the antipoverty programs were entrusted to new organizations believed to have more rapport with the neglected
segment of the population. However, employment service offices continued to have a major role in MDTA
programs and in some EOA programs, although there
were variations among states and areas.

The designation of states and local governments as
prime sponsors changed the role of the employment

service from the presumptive deliverer of manpower
services to one of several agencies that could provide
such services.   Although the U. S. Employment Service
is part of the Manpower Administration, and efforts
have been made on its behalf, the local employment service agencies did not necessarily have the inside track
in competition to become the principal service deliverer.
In 16 of 24 local prime sponsor areas and in one of the
four states in the sample, its role has been reduced.
In two areas, the prime sponsors have eliminated the
employment service from manpower programs.

Under MDTA the employment service was responsible
for classroom and on-the-job training.   In situations in
which that role has been reduced, the major managerial
responsibility for these activities has been taken over by
the prime sponsor, and the employment service has been
left with its supporting role in intake, counseling, and
placement.

The greatest curtailment came in the cities and in
some of the consortia in which alternatives were available and funds were generally tight.   Cutbacks were
most likely to occur where rivalries within the manpower
establishment were sharpest and relationships between
the employment service offices and certain groups in
the population were strained.   Significantly, the employment service role is clearly diminished in every one of
the city prime sponsors studied.   In New York City the
employment service operated MDTA programs before
CETA; it was not awarded a contract in 1975 and employment service staff losses were estimated at 150 positions.
In Philadelphia, the CETA administrator has taken over
the employment service role in the operation of the JOPS
program and has reduced the number of employment service personnel stationed in the CEP office from 33 to
six.   The employment service does have a contract for
training allowance payments.

The employment service role was reduced in six of
the nine consortia studied.   In Kansas City (Kan.), the
prime sponsor chose to assign the core functions to the
OIC and SER on the theory that these organizations are
more effective with groups most in need of manpower
services.   Similarly in Cleveland, where the employment

service had been active in MDTA programs and payment of training allowances, CEP has taken over all activities. However, the employment service does have staff at manpower centers.

CETA administrators reported that they based their decisions to cut back on employment service activities on an assessment of past performance and on relative costs. Such assessments appear to reflect general perceptions rather than formal analysis of performance. They included the belief that the employment service has been insensitive to needs of the disadvantaged, that it has been employer-oriented and not flexible enough to meet the needs of inner-city residents. On the other hand, some employment service officials feel that due consideration was not given to their experience and accomplishments, and that decisions reflect political pressures in situations in which the employment service does not have a constituency.

In some cases the reduced role of the employment service reflects a determination on the part of the CETA administrators to build up their own capability to handle some of the activities formerly managed by the employment service and other organizations. They believe this would give them better control over all facets of the manpower program.

Among the eight prime sponsor areas (most of which are counties) in which the employment service role has been increased, there are fewer alternative agencies and the situation is less competitive. Time pressures made it impractical for the sponsors to develop their own capability or to seek other service deliverers. That employment service personnel were active on the earlier MAPCs and AMPBs and on the present CETA council was undoubtedly a factor. In Pasco (Fla.) and Ramsey (Minn.) counties, the employment service was an expedient choice since there had been virtually no previous manpower activities.

The state programs present a special situation. As prime sponsor the state could be expected to rely more heavily on the state employment security agency. Although the local employment service offices maintained their functions in the balance-of-state programs, it is

significant that the state employment security agency
was not given the major responsibility for the overall
program in any of the four states surveyed.

In Arizona, the governor chose the Department of
Employment Security to handle prime sponsor responsibilities for the balance-of-state program. That department is an umbrella agency encompassing vocational
rehabilitation, welfare, and other units, as well as the
employment service. The key role in North Carolina is
assigned to the Department of Administration; in Texas
to the Department of Community Affairs; and in Maine
to the Office of Manpower Planning and Coordination.
Maine's employment service role in state programs is
virtually the same as before, but in the other three
states changes are expected with the shift of balance-of-
state administration from the state to councils of government and other sub-state organizations.

Local employment service offices sought a larger
role under CETA with varying degrees of enthusiasm.
Some were concerned with protecting staff positions.
Others were committed to the objectives of CETA. Also,
state employment service agencies differed in the amount
of pressure they put on local offices to seek a role in
CETA; some left decisions up to local offices; others
intervened for them. One large state assumed a neutral
position, offering the services that had been rendered
in the past with costs based on past experience. En-
couragement from Manpower Administration regional
offices was spotty, although guidelines had been issued
to employment service offices and training sessions
were held, urging them to maintain their role under
CETA.

Most prime sponsors, unhappy with costs and red
tape, elected not to use the unemployment insurance
system for payment of training allowances. Nine prime
sponsors set up their own payment systems; five arranged for allowance payments through program operators; and two sponsors apparently have elected not to
pay allowances.

A Manpower Administration survey confirms the
reduced employment service role. For the United
States as a whole, a net loss of 700 man years was

reported in activities related to Titles I, II, and VI in
fiscal 1975 compared with man years funded for MDTA
and EOA in fiscal 1974 (6,000 positions in 1974; 5,300
in fiscal 1975). The employment service lost 1,700 positions under Title I, but recovered most of them under
Titles II and VI, according to this survey. 34/ The effects of CETA on the employment service could be pro-
found, not only in terms of reduced staff and resources,
but in the loss of its role as a primary manpower agency
for human resources development.

Implications

The fact the employment service has been sharply
curtailed has significant implications for its manpower
activities in the future. There are signs that the employment service may be returning to its role of serving the
job-ready while CETA serves the disadvantaged. This
would negate the 10-year effort to make the employment
service more responsive to the needs of the disadvantaged.
Firm conclusions at this point would be premature since
there could well be contractual changes in fiscal 1976.
However, if the early trend continues, a two-tier manpower system may emerge: one for the disadvantaged
and another for the better-qualified workers. The employment service is, under the Wagner-Peyser Act, a
manpower institution in its own right. 35/ As such it is
free to compete with CETA program operators for applicants and job openings--this could mean a new round
of duplication. In competing for CETA contracts, some
employment service agencies may improve their effectiveness and enhance their position in the community.

34/ Figures do not include positions supported by transi-
     tion funds provided by the Manpower Administration
     to Employment Service agencies to continue and close
     out categorical projects. If these figures are included,
     there is an overall increase of 850 man years.
35/ The Wagner-Peyser Act, approved in 1933, estab-
     lished the U.S. Employment Service in the Depart-
     ment of Labor and a national system of public
     employment offices operated by states.

PUBLIC VOCATIONAL EDUCATION INSTITUTIONS

In the early 1960s public vocational education institutions began manpower training under the Area Redevelopment Act and later under MDTA. Under those statutes, training needs were identified locally by employment service offices, and classroom training was set up through public vocational education institutions, community colleges, and area technical schools. Since then education agencies have furnished training components of other programs, such as New Careers and Operation Mainstream, and have sponsored work-experience programs for youth.

During the transitional period, assessment of change in the institutional arrangements for skill training and basic education under CETA must be tentative since the classroom-training components were often in disarray. Some MDTA programs continued until the end of December 1974, and new programs had not yet been established. Uncertainty about the amount of vocational education funds from the 5 percent state supplement added to the confusion and delays. With changes in the economy, early plans to establish classroom training programs in some areas gave way to work-experience or public-service employment programs promising more immediate assistance for the unemployed.

By early 1975 a number of trends were emerging. The extent of representation of vocational education agencies on CETA councils appeared to be only slightly less than on the earlier councils. However, the influence of educational officials is less evident on councils that tend to be dominated by the administrator or staff. On balance, the public vocational education agencies are participating in training activities to the same extent as before, but the content and responsibility for training are undergoing changes.

In only six of the 24 local cases studied has the role of public schools or community colleges been reduced in either number of courses or number of enrollees. Three of these cases are cities in which alternative training agencies and facilities are more readily available. In eight cases there has been an increase in training

activities. In balance-of-state programs, public vocational education agencies are well established and are
maintaining their skill-training role. That position
may change as decision making is shifted to subregions.

In almost all prime sponsor areas, public educational
agencies will continue to provide training, and in nearly
all cases, the schools will continue to operate the work-
experience programs. A few sponsors have virtually
eliminated classroom training by public institutions.
In Gary, for instance, the public schools submitted five
proposals, none of which was funded by the city. Private
schools were believed to be more flexible and more capable of tailoring training to specific requirements.

Institutional and political factors contribute to the
extent and nature of vocational education participation in
CETA programs. The influence and prestige of vocational education officials on planning councils is, of
course, a factor in defining the role of vocational education in many areas. The influence of institutional
forces was demonstrated in Philadelphia, where the CETA
administrator, attempting to phase out an established
skill center, ran into opposition from the teachers'
union. The result was a compromise that enabled the
skill center to become more cost competitive through the
state's absorption of administrative costs from its 5
percent fund. In one consortium a county technical institute was given a monopoly on classroom training. This
generated some conflicts, since the facility, located
outside the city, is inaccessible to inner-city trainees
who in the past were served by a community-action
agency. In other cases a shift from public to private
agencies reflects the CETA administrators' desire to
consolidate control over the program.

One of the unexpected effects of CETA is a decline
in importance of skill centers due to a shift to individual
referrals and the transfer of resources to other training
agencies. Prior to CETA eight of the 28 prime sponsor
areas studied had MDTA skill centers and two others
used centers in nearby jurisdictions. In two of the eight
cases, funding of skill centers was reduced. These decisions were based on relative costs, client distances
from skill centers (sometimes in another prime sponsor

area) and alternatives available. In one case the prime
sponsor eliminated the center in favor of individual referral to training, which was easier to handle.

On the whole, local control has not created serious
problems for school systems. Encouraged by state
agencies, school officials submitted proposals to prime
sponsors either for continuing established training programs, setting up new courses, or for placing trainees
on individual referrals. For the most part, arrangements have been made through negotiation rather than
through competitive bidding. About half of the vocational
education officials queried were opposed to competitive
bidding in selecting training agencies. They argue that
prime sponsors should take into account availability of
facilities, qualified instructors, and experience in establishing curricula, as well as costs. One official pointed
out that having to compete from year to year and project
to project would disrupt the orderly management of the
training programs. There was little comment on the
use of private schools for supplemental facilities, a
common practice under MDTA. Some school officials
tend to regard manpower programs as an accommodation
to help the community rather than as a major source of
support for the basic public vocational education system.

Views of public vocational education officials on
whether due consideration was given by prime sponsors
to past performance were mixed. They believed that
when such consideration was given, it was not based on
an objective evaluation but on general perceptions. In
most cases, the schools enjoy a good reputation and were
believed to be capable of continuing to offer effective
manpower training. In the few cases where dissatisfaction was expressed, it was based on the belief that the
vocational education process is too slow and cumbersome
and that training courses, once started, tend to be per-
petuated regardless of need. In some cases, MDTA
courses had lapsed simply for lack of interest and en-
enrollees.

Tension between prime sponsors and vocational
education officials are beginning to surface. The conflicts involve the selection of trainees, performance
standards, and duration of courses. Education officials

complain that trainees are not selected carefully, a
practice that creates problems in trying to integrate
them into courses with better-prepared students. They
also object to what they believe are unrealistic performance standards that require schools to place a certain percentage of enrollees, especially when the schools
are not permitted to screen referrals. There are also
philosophical differences regarding educational objectives. Many educators favor the preparation of students
for broad occupational choices, while manpower officials
seek short, intensive, single-purpose courses to bring
trainees up to job-entry level.

A significant change is taking place in the role of
state educational officials. Formerly, their concurrence
was required in local MDTA classroom-training projects
and they provided support to local school officials. Decisions of this kind are now made by prime sponsors.
The underlying issue, from the educators' point of view,
is the growing influence of nonprofessionals in educational
matters. This, they fear, may tend to lower standards.
The purpose of the 5 percent supplemental vocational
educational fund was to help the state maintain some influence in local programs. The fund is being handled in
different ways and the results have been mixed. In
Maine, where the state has been the only prime sponsor,
the fund is retained at the state level and used for contracts with local schools. In North Carolina, Texas, and
Arizona the fund is distributed to local sponsors for use
at their discretion. In Texas a stipulation that none of
the money may be used for training allowances is being
protested by sponsors. On the whole there is little
control over local use of funds outside the balance-of-
state areas.

Two-thirds of the 24 local prime sponsors plan to
use their 5 percent supplemental funds for classroom
training. Other uses being contemplated were training
allowances, supplemental activities such as adult education and vocational guidance, and in one case, the pur-
chase of equipment.

COMMUNITY-BASED ORGANIZATIONS

By legislative mandate and historical development, community-based organizations (CBOs) have been associated mainly with specially designed work-experience, employability development, and training programs for minority groups, or for disadvantaged members of the labor force. These activities were supported by EOA and MDTA funds on the basis that CBOs provide a bridge to reach minority groups who otherwise would not become involved with establishment institutions. Their programs tended to be innovative and linked to supportive services. Although local in scope, community-based organizations are often affiliated with national organizations and manpower services may be only one of their interests. Prior to CETA contracts for manpower programs were channeled to them directly from the Manpower Administration, with little formal state or local government involvement. However, CBOs usually have local constituencies and a background of relationships with local government officials.

The special role that community-based organizations had played would seem to be precluded by CETA, which prohibits the singling out of specific organizations as presumptive operators. However, the legislative history of CETA supports such recognition and the act explicity endorses a CBO role in several contexts. It mentions services conducted by community-based organizations as one of many types of programs and activites that may be offered. CETA requires that sponsors' plans indicate the arrangements to be made with CBOs to serve the poor. The act also requires that CBOs be represented on the planning council to the extent practicable. There are oblique references such as services for "persons of limited English-speaking ability" and the "need for continued funding of programs of demonstrated effectiveness." Finally, to assist such organizations in their relationships with the prime sponsor, contracts have been awarded to national headquarters of community-based organizations for technical assistance to their local branches.

On the whole, the Urban League, the OIC and SER--
community-based organizations with urban constituencies
among ethnic and racial minorities--are holding their
own or increasing the extent of their services under CETA
in most of the areas studied. In their manpower activities, the Urban League is primarily engaged in arranging
on-the-job training, OIC concentrates on motivational
and skill training, and SER, whose clients are the
Spanish-speaking, emphasizes skill training and English-
as-second-language. Nationally, according to a recent
Manpower Administration report, the funding for these
organizations increased significantly between fiscal 1974
and fiscal 1975.

The Urban League operated programs prior to CETA
in nine of the areas studied; in four of those its services
have expanded. In St. Paul, for example, the Urban
League on-the-job training program is being extended
to take over the role that the employment service played
under MDTA. The Urban League also participates in
the city's manpower center. By contrast, in Gary, despite the good reputation of the Urban League and its
close ties with local government, funding was reduced
in a move to consolidate operations under the city's
management and to avoid duplication of activities.

Table 17. Funds and Local Manpower Projects of
Community Based Organizations, Fiscal Year 1974 and
Fiscal Year 1975

Sponsor[a]/	Local Projects		Funds Contracted	
	FY 1974	FY 1975	FY 1974	FY 1975
			($ million)	($ million)
OIC	101	130	23	37
Urban League	47	75	10	16
SER	42	48	13	21
TOTAL	190	253	46	74

Source: Interchange, Vol. II, No. 7, Manpower
        Administration
a/ Data not available for community action agencies.

In virtually all of the 12 areas where OIC programs operated, they have continued at the same or higher levels. In Philadelphia, OIC's birthplace, and in New York, funding was increased substantially. In Kansas City, OIC and SER have been assigned the core functions for the entire delivery system.

The SER picture is mixed. In five areas, SER has a similar or greater role than it had in 1974, but in two areas the scope of service has been reduced. In Gary, which was served previously from a SER office in East Chicago, its CETA contract limits the activities to recruitment and referral. Basic education and on-the-job skill training, which were formerly offered by SER, will now be provided centrally for all CETA participants.

The biggest controversy involving SER occurred in Austin, significant because the situation there challenges the theoretical basis for the existence of community-based organizations. SER was not re-funded initially because it operation (located in the predominantly Spanish-speaking area) could not be integrated with the prime sponsor's manpower center, and because SER wished to maintain its organizational structure intact. The dispute has encompassed not only the agencies but also the city and county elected officials; it is now in the courts. At issue is whether the approach of separate organizations dealing with the unique problems of individual minority groups is compatible with the concept of a comprehensive delivery system.

Some prime sponsors have preferred to fund new community-based organizations to deal with special enclaves and problems rather than try to force them into a unified system. Others are insisting that community-based organizations must accept eligible clients from all segments of the community as a condition of funding. The implications of this requirement are far-reaching and could affect the independence, identity, and ethnic character of the CBOs.

While the fundamental issue, from the standpoint of the community-based organizations, is how they are integrated into the structure and process of local delivery systems, there are a number of other basic tension points.

One source of tension is their feeling of isolation
from the decision-making process. In several areas,
CBOs are not on the planning council because of possible
conflicts of interest; in another they serve only in a
nonvoting capacity. The most widespread complaint is
the belief of CBOs that they have little actual influence
even if they are on the council.

Additional sources of irritation are the imposition
of performance standards that community-based organizations consider unrealistic and reporting requirements
that they find excessive. Some are also unhappy that the
prime sponsor insists on their serving a broader client
group. This they believe may undermine their attach-
ment to a specific ethnic or racial group.

Although funding of community-based organizations
has increased significantly, there is a general uneasi-
ness about their new role and their difficulty in adjusting
to the prime sponsors' new institutions. They see in
the trend toward consolidation a threat to their identity
and to the rationale for having separate organizations
to deal with specific client groups.

Community-Action Agencies

In 21 of the 28 areas in the sample, community-
action agencies (CAAs) had been engaged in manpower
programs and activities before CETA. In terms of services performed, close to half of the community-action
agencies have a smaller role under CETA. About one-
fourth are expected to continue unchanged, and the remainder will have a bigger piece of the action.

Before CETA, typical community-action agencies
were engaged extensively in work-experience programs
for youth and to a lesser extent for adults. In two cases
in Arizona, community-action agencies operated CEP
programs. Contracts written after CETA were usually
limited to selected manpower services such as outreach, intake, coaching, and followup.

In the 21 prime sponsor areas that had community-
action programs before CETA, 38 separate programs
were identified. Thirteen of these were NYC out-of-school,

eight NYC in-school, and six NYC summer projects. The
rest were programs for adults: Public Service Careers,
Mainstream, and on-the-job training. About one-half
of these programs continued substantially unchanged
under CETA, while about one-third were taken over by
prime sponsors or other operators. So far there have
been two cases in the sample where the local CAA completely lost out under CETA because of the consolidation of delivery systems. In some cases CAAs were not
on the local council, even with a nonvoting status; in
others they were admitted only after protest.

The reasons given in one of the situations where
the CAA lost its contract may be a clue to the problems
CAAs are encountering elsewhere. Beneath the charges
of poor performances and counter-charges of lack of a
proper evaluation system are more fundamental issues.
These include prior adversary relationships and a desire on the part of the CETA administrator to tighten
control of all elements in a comprehensive delivery
system.

As suggested earlier, in some areas the CAAs and
the prime sponsors had different views on who should be
served. The CAAs focused mainly on the minorities
and disadvantaged while the prime sponsors sought to
broaden participation.

Where the role of CAAs has increased, there have
been two main reasons. In some cases, Long Beach
(Cal.) for example, the CAA had a major share of programs before CETA and was in the best position to establish itself under the new administration. In other cases,
the CETA administrator decided to use the expertise of
existing organizations to staff manpower centers and to
extend outreach services to minority communities. In
New York City, the city's manpower administration depends on 26 Neighborhood Manpower Centers of the
Community Corporation. These have assumed greater
significance as intake centers for a variety of programs
under CETA, including referral for Title II and Title VI
public service jobs. However, the fate of these centers
is partially dependent on the CAA to which they are
affiliated.

SUMMARY

Within a framework of changes in the economy and new legislation, prime sponsors were hard-pressed to decide which programs and program operators to retain or change. At the same time, they had to determine questions of the extent of program coordination and integration. The study shows that basically programs are still categorical but that significant developments are occurring.

- For the most part, existing programs in cities, counties, consortia, and balance-of-state areas continued under CETA with the same program operators. However, in many cases the activities performed have been changed to correspond with the prime sponsors' plans.
- There is a significant trend toward the operation of programs directly by prime sponsors. Under CETA the proportion of existing programs in cities, counties, and consortia operated directly by prime sponsors has risen to about one-third.
- The most frequent changes involved the transfer of employment service responsibilities for MDTA institutional training and for on-the-job training to prime sponsors or other operators. The second most frequent changes were the transfers of work-experience programs from community-action agencies to prime sponsors or others. Changes were more common in counties than in cities; consortia showed the least change.
- Significant progress is being made in integrating manpower services at the local level. Most of the prime sponsors in the sample have taken steps toward more integrated programs. Most of the changes occurred in cities, in which consolidation is more manageable. Comprehensive manpower delivery models are being installed in four prime sponsor areas, and mixed systems exist in eleven. In the remaining 13 cases, prime sponsors have chosen to maintain pre-existing programs with only minor changes.

- The planning and operating responsibilities of the employment service are being reduced in a number of local areas but continue unchanged in the balance-of-state programs. The possibility of a two-tier manpower system with the employment service serving the job-ready is beginning to emerge.

- Local vocational education agencies are continuing to provide manpower training with little change, but state vocational education agencies are losing control over local programs. Educators resent the encroachment of nonprofessionals in technical decisions.

- Community-based organizations, generally, have fared well under CETA; community-action agencies, not só well. The tendency toward consolidation is seen by many community-based organizations as a threat to their independence.

6

Program, Before and After

Whether measured in terms of skill acquisition or placement on jobs, the standard manpower programs were considered by some observers to have only limited success in enhancing the employability of those with serious difficulties in finding and keeping jobs. Increased flexibility, it was believed, would enable the prime sponsor to put together the most useful combination of training, work experience, counseling, or other services to give clients more individual attention and more options. This chapter looks at what has happened, compares the kinds of services offered before and after CETA, and examines the reasons for and the effect of the changes.

Congress made clear that it was less concerned with specific programs than with substantive activities. The kinds of services listed in the act[36/] were intended to

36/ The Comprehensive Employment and Training Act, PL 93-203, Section 101, lists these activities: outreach, assessment, referral to appropriate employment or training, orientation, counseling, education and skill training, on-the-job training, services to individuals to enable them to retain employment, supportive services, and transitional public service employment.

underscore a wide range of choices in contrast to the
narrow scope of most categorical programs.

ESTIMATES vs. EXPERIENCE

When the Manpower Administration issued planning
estimates in May 1975 for use in preparing initial Title I
plans, the total resources available for distribution were
below the 1974 funding levels. However, Congress increased the appropriation and the final sum allocated was
12 percent more than in the base year. There were two
unexpected aspects of the initial Title I plans. The first
was the virtual absence of projected expenditures for
public service jobs; it had been assumed that prime sponsors would take advantage of the flexibility permitted by
CETA to use manpower training funds for public service
employment (PSE), but apparently they believed that PSE
funds would be available from other sources. This assumption proved to be correct. Congress extended the
Emergency Employment Act of 1971 in June 1974, and in
December added to CETA a vast new public employment
program (Title VI) in response to growing unemployment.
Second, the plans showed a decrease in the proportion of work-experience programs compared with the
previous year--a decrease more apparent than real.
Close examination revealed that many sponsors, particularly large cities, did not include summer youth work-
experience programs in their 1975 plans. The Manpower
Administration insisted that the summer youth program
must come out of Title I funds since that program was
included in the base figures on which Title I planning ap-
portionments were made. The cities hoped to finance
summer jobs from a separate appropriation as in the
past, or if that failed, from unexpended funds. Prime
sponsors again proved to be right; a separate appropriation for summer employment was passed in June 1975. 37/

37/ The $473 million appropriated included $17 million
     transferred to the Community Services Administra-
     tion for recreation and transportation; $456 million was
     allocated to Title I prime sponsors for summer em-
     ployment programs.

When the 1974 data are adjusted to make the summer youth figures comparable to 1975, the plans of some 400 prime sponsors indicate that about half of Title I participants were to be enrolled in work-experience programs, about the same proportion as in 1974. Classroom training declined from 32 to 29 percent and on-the-job training from 19 to 13 percent (see Table 18).

Before the ink on the plans was dry, it was evident that actual expenditures and enrollments did not correspond with projections because of unrealistic plans and delays in getting started. Moreover, lapsed funds from discontinued categorical programs, consortium incentive money, vocational education 5 percent funds, and in some instances allotments from the state's manpower services fund were tossed in after the initial plans had been drawn up. Thus many sponsors found it possible to add new programs with extra money without reducing existing ones. Other prime sponsors were not able to complete arrangements for the transfer or continuation of activities in accordance with their plans. Most important, the realities of the labor market imposed unexpected new conditions. With the economic decline, on-the-job training openings were evaporating and work-experience programs became increasingly attractive since they are less dependent on the state of the labor market.

The national Title I expenditure and enrollment figures for fiscal 1975 showed the following changes from plans:

- Prime sponsors spent 83 percent of the amount projected--$869 million compared with over $1 billion planned.
- A comparison of planned and actual expenditures and enrollments showed a drift toward work experience from classroom and on-the-job training. The biggest change was in on-the-job training--8 percent of expenditures compared with 15 percent planned and 20 percent spent last year. Expenditures for work-experience activity amounted to 43 percent of the total compared with 35 percent planned for that activity.

Table 18. Percent Distribution of Planned and Actual
Expenditures and Enrollments by Program Activity,
CETA Title I, U. S. Total, Fiscal Year 1975, and for
Comparable Programs in Fiscal Year 1974

Program Activity	Funds			Enrollments		
	FY 1974 Obliga-tions[a]	FY 1975 Expenditures		FY 1974 Enroll-ments[a]	FY 1975 Enroll-ments	
		Planned[b]	Ac-tual		Planned[b]	Ac-tual
Class-room training	40	34	30	32	29	28
On-the-job training	20	15	8	19	13	7
Public ser-vice em-ployment	-	5	7	-	2	3
Work ex-perience	38	35	43	49	48	54
Service to clients and other ac-tivities	2	11	11	NA	8	8
ALL ACTIVI-TIES	100	100	100	100	100	100

Source: Computed from Manpower Administration data.
a/ Excludes summer youth programs (comparable to
    part of Title III of CETA) and Emergency Employ-
    ment Act (comparable to Titles II and VI). See
    Appendix B Table 7.
b/ As of October 1974.
(Details may not add to totals due to rounding.)

- Corresponding changes were reflected in enrollment figures. Only 35 percent were enrolled in
  training activities compared with 42 percent
  planned; 54 percent were in work experience compared with 48 percent planned for that activity.

PROGRAM MIX IN SAMPLE AREAS

The new emphasis toward work experience was reflected in the sample areas studied. On the whole initial plans tended to continue business as usual, reflecting tight deadlines, the influence of existing program operators, and the inexperience of CETA administrators and staff.

Most of the prime sponsors expected to receive less funds than their areas had received in 1974. When the revised allocations came out, however, 15 prime sponsors had more Title I funds than the 1974 base amount and 13 had less. Prime sponsors with more funds to spend, mostly counties and consortia, were in a position to expand all of the prior year's programs and activities with only minor changes in emphasis. Others had to consider some reductions.

There are significant differences in program combinations by type of prime sponsor. Cities are using the largest proportion of funds and enrollees for classroom training, while the counties, consortia, and states are devoting the biggest share to work-experience programs (Table 19).

Decisions regarding the appropriate program combinations were generally not based on analysis of labor market conditions and needs of clients, or on performance of program deliverers. Rather they were heavily conditioned by the kind of programs that prime sponsors inherited and were familiar with--skill training and work experience. Lack of knowledge of alternatives and time pressures constrained the decision-making process. Consequently, the continuation of existing patterns was the rule. Cities tended to emphasize classroom training because of the availability of classrooms and teachers. Counties, consortia, and balance-of-state sponsors preferred work experience because of ease of administration. In most cases existing programs were re-funded with the same operators or were transferred to prime sponsors who continued to operate them with little change.

The early findings of this study do not support the premise that local authorities, given the opportunity, would refashion manpower programs to correspond more

Table 19. Percent Distribution of Expenditures and Enrollments by Program Activity and by Type of Sponsor, CETA Title I, Sample Prime Sponsors, Fiscal Year 1975

Type of Sponsor	Total	Program Activity				
		Classroom Training	On-the-job Training	Public Service Employment	Work Experience	Services and Other
Expenditures						
City	100	44	9	a/	27	19
County	100	34	7	4	38	18
Consortium	100	26	7	5	48	14
Balance of State	100	22	6	10	57	5
Enrollments b/						
City	100	46	8	a/	27	19
County	100	41	6	2	51	-
Consortium	100	33	4	1	55	7
Balance of State	100	19	9	6	66	1

Source: Computed from Manpower Administration data.
a/ Less than 0.5 percent.
b/ Clients enrolled in more than one activity may be
   counted in each. Participants who are given manpower services only are not counted as enrolled.
(Details may not add to totals due to rounding.
Figures are averages of percentages.)

closely to the needs of the local scene. However, there are some developments that may become significant. One is the emerging of service-type activities in some areas.[38] St. Paul is the outstanding example, but several other prime sponsors are devoting a sizable proportion of their resources to such activities as counseling, assessment,

38/ Manpower Administration reports show expenditures but not enrollments for "service" activities. For that reason it is difficult to follow trends in these activities.

and direct job placement as distinguished from training
and employability development.

Changes are also being made in the content of programs as the influence of local CETA administrators
and advisory councils begins to penetrate. In several
areas there has been a tendency to emphasize basic education and motivational training to meet what are perceived to be the needs of clientele. Gary, for example,
stresses pre-vocational training in an effort to prepare
clients to participate successfully in on-the-job or vocational training. Other areas are stressing referral
based upon individual client need rather than simply
directing participants to whatever programs are available at the time.

New programs for special groups were reported in
a number of areas. For example, the Lansing, San
Joaquin, and St. Petersburg consortia have pilot projects
for such groups as ex-offenders, alcoholics, drug addicts,
migratory farm workers, and older workers. Innovative
techniques are being attempted in a few cases. In Long
Beach (Cal.), a modular, self-paced skill training program is being installed. Arizona gives selected participants vouchers that permit them to shop for training on
a reimbursable basis. Still, such new approaches are
not widespread. Prime sponsors have generally taken
a cautious approach during the first year. As for 1976,
some prime sponsors are talking of innovations, but
most expect to continue the same activities.

Rigidities built in the first year are likely to persist.
Yet there are indications that the potential for change is
present. Innovative forces include: 1) the involvement
of more groups in the planning process; 2) closer access
by community groups to the decision makers; 3) introduction of manpower programs in areas in which few or
none had existed; and 4) increased outreach, counseling,
coaching, and other services suggesting more responsive-
ness to individual problems.

Once program changes are decided upon, they can
be implemented more expeditiously than before. The
previous system that worked through 17 programs, each
funded separately through an annual appropriations, budget, and grant cycle, made it very difficult to respond to

changes in a timely fashion. Under CETA, the single
grant makes it possible to adjust programs quickly at
the local level based on a firsthand review of developments on the scene.

Where subcontractors are used, the prime sponsor's
freedom is necessarily limited. Moreover, when major
changes are involved, there is the inevitable modifica-
tion procedure, requiring approval by the regional office
of the Manpower Administration. On balance, however,
prime sponsors have been able to adjust more quickly
to changed economic conditions than was possible under
the pre-CETA structure.

SUMMARY

Experience during the turbulent first year indicates
that:

- Prime sponsors, by and large, planned to maintain a pattern of programs similar to earlier
  years, with less emphasis on classroom and on-
  the-job training and slightly more on work experience. Cities tend to favor classroom training
  while other types of sponsors put more emphasis
  on work-experience projects. The influence of
  sponsors and councils is reflected in changes in
  the content of training although few major innovations have been made. In some cases a shift
  toward more service-type activity is noticeable,
  but this may be due in part to a revised system
  of reporting.
- Program expenditures and enrollments during
  fiscal 1975 did not correspond to plans. A marked
  decline in on-the-job training and an increase in
  work experience reflect the impact of the recession.
- When changes are indicated, prime sponsors can
  respond more quickly than was possible under the
  pre-CETA categorical programs. However,
  prime sponsors may be constrained by their own
  administrative procedures and councils and by
  the necessity of working within the existing institutional structure.

7

The Participants

Since only a fraction of those who need local manpower services can be served with the resources available at any given time, deciding who will be accommodated
becomes very important. During fiscal 1974, 2.6 million
individuals were enrolled in all Department of Labor
funded manpower programs, including the Work Incentive Program (WIN), the Job Corps, the Emergency
Employment Act (EEA), and others not under the comprehensive manpower umbrella. The number enrolled
in programs corresponding with CETA Title I was
approximately 800,000 in fiscal 1974, excluding summer
programs for youth; and about 1.4 million if summer
youth programs are included. [39]/
The clientele of manpower development programs
prior to CETA was predominantly the disadvantaged--by
law and by social policy--except for the temporary EEA
program. Economic Opportunity Act (EOA) programs
were exclusively for the unemployed and underemployed
in families that were defined as living in poverty. Under
MDTA the policy was to select two-thirds of the participants from the disadvantaged population.
The Comprehensive Employment and Training Act
(CETA), on the other hand, is more ambiguous and is

[39]/ See Appendix B, Table 7

open to broad interpretation. The term "economically disadvantaged" does appear in the preamble, but so do the terms "unemployed" and "underemployed" persons without qualification. The opening paragraph of Title I refers vaguely to "individuals" in need of help in securing employment. Eligibility requirements are again hinted at in a section requiring prime sponsors to assure that services will be provided to those "most in need, " but this is qualified by the phrase "to the maximum extent feasible. "40/ Congress, in an attempt to carry water on both shoulders, left to prime sponsors the responsibility for setting eligibility specifications under Title I within the broad guidelines in the act and in consultation with local advisory councils. The question then is what effect decentralization of decision making is having on the kind of clientele enrolled in manpower programs. This chapter reviews the experience of prime sponsors in identifying groups most in need and selecting clients to be served under Title I. The effect of changes in the delivery system on the flow of clients and on the services provided to them is also considered.

NUMBER AND CHARACTERISTICS OF PARTICIPANTS

Most prime sponsors in the sample projected more enrollees than the number actually served in categorical

40/ References in this paragraph are to Public Law 93-203, Sections 2, 101, and 105(a)(1). Under Title II consideration must be given to those longest unemployed, to Vietnam-era veterans, and to persons who have participated in manpower training programs. Title VI gives preferred consideration in public service jobs to persons who have exhausted or who are not eligible for unemployment insurance benefits, as well as to those unemployed for 15 or more weeks. Recognition of the special needs of target groups is also found in Title III of the Act which authorizes federal programs for Indians, migrant and seasonal farmworkers, as well as for youth, offenders, older workers, persons of limited English-speaking ability, and others with labor market disadvantages.

programs in 1974. Manpower Administration reports
appear to confirm these estimates. In fiscal 1975,
1,125,000 individuals were served under Title 1, ex-
ceeding the 1974 total of 800,000 in comparable pro-
grams.41/   Reporting practices that permit counting as
individuals served those who receive only minimal manpower services, without being enrolled in training or
work experience programs, may account in part for the
increase.

Planning guidelines required prime sponsors to list
priority target groups, but those listings had little mean-
ing. Listings were prepared in great haste, before the
newly designated prime sponsors had an opportunity to
become aware of community needs or consult their advisory councils. Labor market and demographic information was not specific enough to be useful, nor did a
standard list or criteria exist for identifying target
groups. The result was a melange of terms. Moreover,
the policies set by CETA administrators were not always
followed by those selecting program participants. The
pressure of the newly unemployed and other groups facing
hardships in a loose labor market upset plans and priorities.

Virtually all sponsor plans recognize the disadvantaged as a priority group. Nevertheless, the study found
that a broader socioeconomic group is being admitted to
Title I programs as a result of pressures at the local
level as well as the changing economic climate. In nine
of the 28 prime sponsor areas studied, a trend toward
different, possibly less disadvantaged, participants has
been noted. Among the reasons are:

The Legislation Eligibility requirements under Title I
give considerable discretion to prime sponsors and invite a loose definition of groups to be served. There is

41/ The 1,125,000 does not include summer employees
    (545,000 in the summer of 1974) who were funded
    separately. Enrollees carried over in categorical
    programs (193,000 at end of September) were not
    added to avoid duplication as some of these were
    transferred to Title I programs.

a tendency to accommodate a more diversified population including additional women, older workers, Spanish-
speaking persons, heads of households, and newly unemployed persons. The loosening of elibigility criteria is
being interpreted as opening up programs to less disadvantaged unemployed persons. In one county, for example, officials are emphazing the unemployed who receive
no financial aid. They feel that the pre-CETA programs
had too narrow a focus and that limiting manpower services exclusively to the economically disadvantaged is
not equitable.

The Allocation Formula Many suburban counties formerly within the orbit of cities are now prime sponsors
themselves. Predictably, their program participants
reflect the characteristics of the county populations--
more whites, fewer disadvantaged. The fact that Title I
grants to counties have been significantly higher than
last year reinforces this change.

Decisions to Widen Participation Even in cities with
large minority populations and established community-
based organizations, an attempt is being made to require CBOs to serve a wider spectrum including the
disadvantaged of all races and the victims of the recession. In Topeka, for example, CETA is having a major
impact on the kind of client groups served by community-
based organizations. Prior to CETA both SER and OIC
were identified almost exclusively with Mexican-American
and black communities. Under CETA, the clientele of
SER is reported to be less than 50 percent Spanish-
American.

Program Mix Decisions to change the kinds of programs
offered may affect the selection of the client population.
In North Carolina, for example, emphasis on skill training in preference to work-experience programs in the
prime sponsor's plan was justified as a means of raising
skill levels, but was viewed by some as an attempt to
reach more qualified applicants.

Change in the Economy   The increase in unemployment
has swelled the ranks of those seeking admission to manpower programs in competition with the disadvantaged
clientele usually served.   A number of prime sponsors
are emphasizing priority for unemployed heads of
households, although the disadvantaged may have
preference within that category.

The Reward System   The emphasis on performance in
evaluations and in contracting for the delivery of manpower services favors the selection of applicants likely
to succeed rather than those most in need.

    There are however, forces tending to resist change
and maintain the pre-CETA client mix.   The fact that
community-based organizations and client representatives constitute close to one-third of the membership on
planning councils may be significant, although the
strength of the influence of these groups in the councils
is open to question.   In some areas, the personal commitment of the CETA administrator and staff assures
consideration of minorities and the disadvantaged.   The
location of intake centers affects the kind of clients
selected.   Inner-city centers attract minority clients.
Regional Manpower Administration offices are also encouraging the selection of disadvantaged clients.

    Control over the selection and referral process is
a key element in determining the composition of CETA
clients.   Where the CETA administrator has contracted
out this function, he has less direct control over the
selection of clients.   In cases in which enrollment responsibilities for on-the-job training have been moved
from the employment service to community-based organizations, more of the disadvantaged are likely to be
served.   On the other hand, if prime sponsors have taken
over activities formerly handled by community-action
agencies, the client mix may move in the other direction.

    Manpower Administration reports of clients served
under Title I during fiscal 1975 reflect a trend toward
more highly qualified participants compared to clients
in similar categorical programs in fiscal 1975 (Table 20):

Table 20.   Characteristics of CETA Title I Participants,
U. S. Total, Second, Third, and Fourth Quarters, Fiscal
Year 1975, Compared with Participants of Similar Cate-
gorical Programs, Fiscal Year 1974 (percentages)

	Fiscal Year 1974[a]	Fiscal Year 1975 (Cumulative)		
Characteristics		Second Quarter	Third Quarter	Fourth Quarter
Sex: Male	57. 7	50. 6	53. 1	54. 4
Female	42. 3	49. 4	46. 9	45. 6
Age: 21 and				
under	63. 1	65. 4	57. 5	61. 7
22 - 44	30. 5	28. 3	35. 2	32. 1
45 and				
over	6. 2	6. 4	7. 3	6. 1
Education:				
8 grades or				
less	15. 1	13. 8	12. 6	13. 3
9 - 11	51. 1	53. 5	47. 7	47. 6
12 and over	33. 6	32. 7	39. 8	39. 1
Economically				
disadvantaged	86. 7	80. 7	75. 8	77. 3
Race: White	54. 9	52. 4	57. 2	54. 6
Black	37. 0	40. 5	36. 1	38. 5
Other	8. 1	7. 1	6. 4	6. 9[c]
Spanish				
American	15. 4	12. 1	13. 4	12. 5
Veterans	15. 3	8. 0	10. 2	9. 6
Labor Force				
Status:				
Employed	7. 6[b]	2. 7	2. 9	2. 3
Underem-				
ployed	8. 7[b]	4. 6	4. 7	4. 5
Unemployed	75. 6[b]	56. 1	64. 8	61. 6
Not in labor				
force	8. 1[b]	36. 6	27. 6	31. 6

Source: Manpower Administration
a/ Includes MDTA-inst. , JOP, NYC in-school, NYC out-
    of-school, Mainstream, CEP, and JOBS.
b/ Excludes NYC in-school and JOBS enrollees
c/ Includes Puerto Ricans, not classified by race.

- The proportion of economically disadvantaged has dropped markedly from 87 percent in comparable programs in 1974 to 77 percent under CETA.
- Those who had completed high school rose from 34 percent to 39 percent, another reflection of less disadvantaged clientele.
- Minorities represent a slightly smaller proportion under CETA. (The proportion of American Indians is down sharply, but this is due to their enrollment in separate programs for Indians under Title III.)
- The proportion of veterans dropped significantly.

Figures for the first year are still preliminary and are affected to a large extent by clients transferred from pre-CETA programs. The full impact of CETA will not be known for some time. However, a comparison of Title I data for the second, third, and fourth quarters of fiscal 1975 reinforces the basic trend: higher proportions of men, whites, persons of prime working age, the better educated, the less disadvantaged, and persons who were unemployed rather than underemployed prior to entry in programs.

CHARACTERISTICS OF TITLE I PARTICIPANTS BY TYPE OF SPONSOR

As expected, there are significant variations in the characteristics of CETA Title I participants by type of prime sponsors. Manpower Administration reports for the second quarter of fiscal 1975 show the highest proportion of females and blacks in cities. The balance-of-state programs reported the highest proportion of white clients, youth, persons with less than a high school education, and those not in the labor force, reflecting an emphasis on youth work-experience programs (Table 21).

The difference between cities and counties is particularly interesting. Counties tend to have an older, better-educated, and less disadvantaged clientele. The proportion of black clients is far lower in counties than in cities, but still relatively high considering the smaller minority population in suburban counties.

Table 21. Characteristics, CETA Title I Participants,
U. S. Total by Type of Prime Sponsor, Second Quarter,
Fiscal Year 1975[a/] (percentages)

| Characteristics | Total | Type of Prime Sponsor | | | |
		City	County	Consor-tium	Balance of State
Sex: Male	50. 6	46. 8	49. 4	51. 4	52. 1
Female	49. 4	53. 2	50. 6	48. 6	47. 9
Age: 21 and under	65. 3	64. 2	59. 7	60. 9	76. 1
22 - 44	28. 3	30. 6	33. 0	31. 8	18. 8
45 and over	6. 4	5. 2	7. 3	7. 3	5. 1
Education: 8 grades or less	13. 8	10. 5	11. 3	14. 0	16. 8
9 - 11	53. 5	53. 5	49. 7	51. 0	59. 3
12 and over	32. 7	36. 0	39, 0	35. 0	23. 9
Race: White	52. 4	24. 6	53. 1	53. 8	63. 4
Black	40. 5	68. 3	38. 6	40. 5	27. 8
Other	7. 1	6. 1	8. 3	5. 7	8. 8
Economically disadvantaged	80. 7	83. 4	69. 8	83. 0	82. 3
Labor Force Status: Employed	2. 7	2. 5	3. 8	2. 8	1. 9
Underem-ployed	4. 6	4. 6	5. 3	4. 7	3. 9
Unemployed	56. 1	73. 0	61. 4	59. 2	39. 7
Not in labor force	36. 6	19. 9	29. 5	33. 3	54. 9

Source: Manpower Administration, U. S. Dept. of Labor
a/ Cumulative through December 31, 1974

Characteristics of Participants in Sample Areas

The aggregate figures disguise wide variations
among individual prime sponsors (Table 22). 42/
Differences are due to demographic characteristics of
the population, priorities in the selection of enrollees,
as well as to the kinds of programs offered. Reporting
problems may also be involved, particularly in classi-
fication of "races. "

Table 22. Characteristics of CETA Title I Participants,
Sample Prime Sponsor Areas, Fiscal Year 1975

Characteristics	Range	Median
	(Percent)	(Percent)
Female	37 - 57	46
Age: 21 and under	37 - 74	59
45 and over	2 - 16	5
Education: 8 years or less	3 - 21	11
12 years or more	22 - 71	40
Economically disadvantaged	52 - 99	77
Black	1 - 86	38
Spanish-speaking	0 - 47	11
Veterans	2 - 19	9

Source: Computed from Manpower Administration data.

Minorities, because of their economic status, are
more heavily represented in manpower programs than
their proportion of the total population would warrant.
Cook County (Ill.) reports an extreme situation: about
60 percent of the enrollees are black although they
constitute less than 4 percent of the county population,
this may be due to the heavy selection of trainees from
minority areas. In Gary, whose population is more

42/ See also Appendix B, Table 10.

than 50 percent black, virtually all participants are
black and economically disadvantaged. Other areas
with high black enrollments are Philadelphia, Raleigh,
New York, and Cleveland.

The Orange County (Cal.), Phoenix-Maricopa, and
San Joaquin (Cal.) consortia have the highest proportion of Spanish-speaking enrollees, reflecting of course,
the high proportion of Spanish-speaking persons in
those areas. Other areas in the sample with high proportions of Spanish-speaking enrollees are Austin and
the balance of Texas.

FLOW OF CLIENTS THROUGH THE SYSTEM

Some indication of the kinds of services being offered to clients may be gleaned from the way in which
they enter and move through the manpower delivery
system. CETA was expected to enable local communities to provide more options to the client by better use
of available resources and expertise.

The flow of clients through the manpower system
is related to the degree of program integration (see
Chapter 5). Those prime sponsors who have set up comprehensive systems, established central points for receiving clients, or arranged for close cooperation among
programs in a unified referral system have more sus-
tained contact with participants from entry to followup
than those that have continued the categorical approach
of separate programs.

The St. Paul delivery system comes closest to a
comprehensive model (see p. 102). An adult entering the
Career Guidance and Training Center is given a battery
of services, including aptitude and interest assessment,
vocational guidance, and referral to either on-the-job
or instututional training or to counseling. Arrangements
are made for supportive services if necessary. The
center remains responsible for the client through all
stages to final placement. Youth are handled separately
in a Youth Career Exploration and Employment Project
that arranges for part-time work-experience and summer youth opportunities as well as career counseling

and education. This system places more stress on services than on training and employability development.

In most prime sponsors' areas, however, the entry channels continue to be through separate categorical programs. In Topeka, for example, there is no central coordination; each program selects its own trainees (with the exception of the skill center, whose trainees are selected by SER) and provides the same services as formerly.

Some prime sponsors have increased the fragmentation of service by adding more categorical programs. Before CETA, Lorain County (Oh.) used the employment service exclusively for the selection and referral of adults to MDTA institutional training. Upon completion of training the clients returned to the employment service for placement. Youth were directed to the community-action agency for summer jobs. Under CETA, the entire system has become less integrated. The community-action agency, the employment service, and the prime sponsor all perform outreach; the employment service and the prime sponsor share intake activities. A client may be assessed and tested at several different agencies. Job development and placement are carried on separately by three different agencies. The entire system has become more complex from the standpoint of participants.

Between categorical programs (each with a limited range of services and training options) and a comprehensive design, are many intermediate arrangements. A number of areas have now or are planning central intake centers. Neighborhood Manpower Centers established by New York City before CETA have become intake centers for variety of CETA programs. In Philadelphia, the city's manpower staff have established six outreach centers to decentralize the reception activities of its central CEP facility. Other programs, however, continue to provide services for their clients outside the manpower centers. Gary has six centers to handle counseling, coaching, training referral, and placement. Thus there appears to be a trend toward the development of comprehensive centers, but many

separate arrangements with individual programs are
still operative. In a few cases, centers are providing
a full range of services, while in others, they are merely
intake points; clients are referred to other agencies for
basic services. Another variation of a mixed system
calls for functional specialization among program operators. Responsibility for the client, although transferred from one agency to another, is clearly assigned
through specific contractual arrangements.

It is too early to determine whether these attempts
to coordinate the handling of clients will be successful.
There are a number of obstacles. Program operators
frequently resist curtailment of functions. The relationships between referral and training agencies are sometimes less than harmonious, particularly where the
training agencies are not required to accept referrals
from the manpower center or from other agencies. The
resulting friction may adversely affect service to the
client. Finally, inexperience may make it more difficult to provide adequate manpower services. Some
manpower practitioners have noted that the advantages
of consolidating functions may be offset by the problems
that result when a range of client services formerly
provided in a single agency are now available only in
separate locations.

SUMMARY

The effect of some decategorization and the transfer
of decision making is beginning to be felt in both selection of clients and in the manner in which they are
handled in the system:

- There is a trend toward serving a broader economic group of clients and a weakening of forces
  that have concentrated manpower programs on
  the disadvantaged. Factors associated with this
  trend are the spread of programs to the suburbs,
  the conscious policy of prime sponsors to extend
  the client base, the change in eligibility requirements, and the reshuffling of program content.

- The decline in the economy is having an impact on the selection of clients. The shift toward enrollment of adult heads of households and the recently unemployed reflects this trend.
- On the other hand, there are institutional factors operating to maintain pre-CETA client composition. In most areas pre-CETA program operators continue to conduct their own programs and in some cases their scope of activity has been enlarged. Previous practices under categorical programs will inevitably affect the selection of participants.
- In a number of areas the process of recruiting, counseling, and placing participants is handled by separate program operators substantially as before. In a few cases an attempt is being made to install a comprehensive system tailored to the individual; elsewhere the system is partially coordinated. During the first year under CETA prime sponsors have had difficulty in attempting to integrate or reorganize the flow of clients through the system.

Appendix A

Manpower Acronyms

Manpower Legislation

CETA	Comprehensive Employment and Training Act of 1973
EOA	Economic Opportunity Act of 1964
EEA	Emergency Employment Act of 1971
MDTA	Manpower Development and Training Act of 1962
EJUAA	Emergency Jobs and Unemployment Assistance Act of 1974

Planning Systems

AMPB	Ancillary Manpower Planning Board
BOS/MPC	Balance of State Manpower Planning Council (CETA)
CAMPS	Cooperative Area Manpower Planning System
MPC	Local Manpower Planning Council (CETA)
MAPC	Manpower Area Planning Council (pre-CETA)
SMPC	State Manpower Planning Council (pre-CETA)
SMSC	State Manpower Services Council (CETA)

Manpower Programs

CEP	Concentrated Employment Program
JOP	Jobs Optional Program (MDTA-OJT)
NYC	Neighborhood Youth Corps
JOBS	Job Opportunities in the Business Sector - National Alliance of Businessmen
OJT	On-the-Job Training
OIC	Opportunities Industrialization Center
PEP	Public Employment Program (under EEA)
PSC	Public Service Careers Program (includes New Careers)
PSE	Public Service Employment
SER	Services, Employment, Redevelopment (Spanish-speaking, self-help organization)

| UL | Urban League |
| WIN | Work Incentive Program (training for welfare recipients) |

Governmental Units

BOS	Balance of State
CAA	Community-Action Agency
CBO	Community-Based Organization
COG	Council of Governments
MA	Manpower Administration (DOL)
OEO	Office of Economic Opportunity (now Community Services Administration)
RO	Regional Office, U. S. Department of Labor
ES	State Employment Security Agency (also local employment service office)
DHEW	U. S. Department of Health, Education and Welfare
DOL	U. S. Department of Labor
VOED	Vocational Education Agency

Appendix B
Statistical Tables

TABLE 1 Selected Data for Sample Prime Sponsor Areas

Type and Class of Prime Sponsor	Population 1970	Percent of Total Population				Families Below Poverty		Unemployment 1973	
		Rural	Negro	Other Races	Spanish Heritage	Number	Percent of Total Families	Number	Unemployment Rate
	(1)	(2)	(3)	(4)	(5)	(6)	(7)	(8)	(9)
I Cities									
A. Pop. less than 1 mill. U.R.[1] less than 6.5%									
St. Paul, Minn.	309,828	—	3.5	1.1	2.1	4,776	6.4	7,552	5.0
Topeka, Kans.	125,011	—	8.4	1.2	4.7	2,353	7.3	2,159	3.7
Gary, Ind.	175,415	—	53.8	0.5	8.1	5,135	12.3	3,601	5.1
	610,254	—	18.7	0.9	4.4	12,264	8.2	13,312	4.8
B. Pop. less than 1 mill. U.R. 6.5% or more									
Long Beach. Cal.	358,633	—	5.3	2.9	7.3	7,620	8.2	10,110	6.6
C. Pop. 1 mill. or more U.R. less than 6.5%									
New York, N.Y.	7,894,862	—	21.1	2.3	10.3	236,507	11.5	190,651	6.0
D. Pop. 1 mill. or more U.R. 6.5% or more									
Philadelphia, Pa.	1,948,609	—	33.6	0.8	1.4	53,705	11.2	51,700	6.8
TOTAL	10,812,358	—	22.7	1.9	8.2	310,096	11.2	265,772	6.1

II Counties

A. Pop. less than 1 mill. U.R. less than 6.5%

Middlesex, N.J.	583,813	4.6	4.4	0.5	1.9	5,931	4.0	15,664	5.6
Union, N.J.*	430,403	0.0	10.0	0.4	0.4	4,007	3.5	7,999	4.1
Ramsey, Minn.*	166,522	0.9	0.4	0.6	0.7	1,076	2.7	2,989	3.9
Chester, Pa.	278,311	55.0	7.6	0.5	0.5	3,021	4.5	4,237	3.4
Calhoun, Mich.	141,963	40.4	8.4	0.4	1.2	2,700	7.5	3,791	5.8
Lorain, Ohio	256,843	14.4	6.4	0.5	4.0	3,617	5.7	5,572	3.9
	1,857,855	14.8	6.4	0.5	1.5	20,352	4.3	40,252	4.6

B. Pop. less than 1 mill. U.R. 6.5% or more

Stanislaus, Cal.	194,506	30.1	0.9	1.7	12.6	6,002	11.8	11,355	11.3
Pasco, Fla.	108,865[2]	66.2	4.9	0.3	1.5	4,281	17.5	2,238	7.3
	303,371	40.1	2.1	1.4	9.5	10,283	13.7	13,593	10.4

C. Pop. 1 mill. or more U.R. less than 6.5%

Cook, Ill.*	2,125,412	0.9	3.9	0.5	1.9	16,587	3.0	37,614	3.6
TOTAL	4,286,638	9.5	4.9	0.6	2.2	47,222	4.3	91,459	4.4

III Consortia

A-B. Pop. less than 1 mill.

Lansing, Mich.	378,423	30.5	3.9	0.7	2.2	5,466	6.1	7,483	4.4
Phoenix/Maricopa, Ariz.	967,522	6.6	3.4	2.1	14.5	21,818	8.9	19,117	4.0
Raleigh, N.C.	350,211	45.9	22.7	0.4	0.3	12,912	14.6	5,035	2.8
San Joaquin, Cal.	290,208	23.1	5.4	6.5	18.0	8,179	11.2	11,137	8.5
St. Petersburg, Fla.	522,329	3.8	8.2	0.3	1.0	13,903	9.0	6,436	2.9
Austin, Tex.	443,035	24.5	11.4	0.9	16.0	16,320	15.3	5,545	2.5
Kansas City, Ka.	186,845	8.0	19.1	0.7	3.0	4,643	9.6	2,884	3.4
	3,138,573	17.5	8.7	1.6	9.1	83,241	10.3	57,637	3.2

C-D. Pop. 1 mill. or more

Cleveland, Ohio	1,981,477	4.1	16.8	0.5	1.1	35,160	7.0	34,745	4.1
Orange County, Ca.	1,420,386	1.1	0.7	2.0	11.3	18,608	5.2	36,100	5.2
	3,401,863	2.0	10.1	1.6	5.3	53,768	6.2	70,845	4.6
TOTAL	6,540,436	9.9	9.4	1.3	7.1	137,009	8.1	128,482	4.2

TABLE 1 (Continued)

Type and Class of Prime Sponsor	Population 1970	Percent of Total Population				Families Below Poverty		Unemployment 1973	
		Rural	Negro	Other Races	Spanish Heritage	Number	Percent of Total Families	Number	Unemployment Rate
IV States and Bal. of States									
A-B. Pop. less than 1 mill.									
Maine	992,048	49.2	0.3	0.4	0.4	25,622	10.3	25,200	5.9
Arizona*	453,293	54.6	2.1	17.7	24.2	19,037	18.1	8,983	5.1
	1,445,341	50.9	0.9	5.9	7.9	44,659	12.6	34,183	5.7
C-D. Pop. 1 mill. or more									
North Carolina*	3,188,705	69.5	22.3	1.3	0.2	151,419	18.7	57,501	3.8
Texas*	3,231,598	42.5	14.6	0.5	12.6	147,973	17.7	54,660	3.7
	6,420,303	55.9	18.5	0.9	6.4	299,392	18.2	112,161	3.6
TOTAL	7,865,644	55.0	15.2	1.8	6.7	344,051	17.2	143,344	4.4
TOTAL SAMPLE	29,505,076	18.2	15.2	1.6	6.7	838,378	11.1	629,058	5.0

Source: U.S. Census, 1970, and Manpower Administration, U.S. Department of Labor
[1] U.R.—unemployment rate
[2] Revised in 1973
*Balance of County or State

TABLE 2 Federal Obligations for Work and Training Programs Administered by the Department of Labor, Selected Fiscal Years 1963–1974 (amounts in thousands)

Manpower Programs	FY 1974 (1)	FY 1972 (2)	FY 1970 (3)	FY 1968 (4)	FY 1966 (5)	FY 1963–1964 (6)
Total	$2,143,613[1]	$2,696,940	$1,418,552	$802,173	$628,407	$198,181
Manpower Development & Training Act	398,462	424,553	336,580	296,418	339,649	198,181
Institutional Training	307,896	355,708	287,031	221,847	281,710	190,744
JOP-OJT[2]	90,566	68,845	49,549	74,571	57,939	7,437
Neighborhood Youth Corps	661,712	517,244	356,589	281,864	263,337	—
In School	88,570	74,897	59,242	58,908	3	—
Out of School	113,651	121,962	97,923	96,279	3	—
Summer	459,491	320,385	199,424	126,677	—	—
Operation Mainstream	114,664	85,164	51,043	22,319	—	—
Public Service Careers	28,334	58,301	89,366	7,557	—	—
Special Impact[4]	—	—	—	2,038	—	—
Concentrated Employment Program	146,489[5]	154,602	187,592	93,057	25,421	—
Jobs (Federally Financed)	64,026	118,224	148,820	89,920	—	—
Work Incentive Program	250,127	174,788	78,780	9,000	—	—
Job Corps	149,551	202,185	169,782	—	—	—
Public Employment Program	281,120[6]	961,879	—	—	—	—

Source: Manpower Reports of the President, 1970–75

[1] Includes $39,127,612 obligated for the Migrants Program and $10 million for Title IX, National Older Workers Program, which are not shown separately.

[2] Includes the JOBS-Optional Program (JOP), which began in fiscal 1971, and the MDTA on-the-job (OJT) program, which ended in fiscal 1970 except for national contracts. Also includes Construction Outreach.

[3] Data are not available for NYC components prior to fiscal 1967.

[4] Transferred to the Office of Economic Opportunity, July 1, 1969.

[5] Total includes $36,775,542 in Comprehensive Manpower Program allocations for FY 1974 only.

[6] Includes $44,010,000 under Title II and $237,110,000 under Title III-A of CETA (extension of Emergency Employment Act).

(Details may not add to totals due to rounding.)

TABLE 3 CETA Title II and Emergency Employment Act Allocations, Fiscal Year 1974, CETA Titles II and VI Allocations, Fiscal Year 1975, Sample Prime Sponsors (amounts in thousands)

| | | Title II | | | | Title VI FY 1975 | |
| | EEA FY 1974 Allocation | FY 1974 | | FY 1975 | | | |
Prime Sponsor		Formula Allocation	Total[1]	Formula Allocation	Total[1]	Formula Allocation	Total[1]
	(1)	(2)	(3)	(4)	(5)	(6)	(7)
	$27,530.0	$39,529.8	$45,496.6	$37,054.7	$44,029.1	$121,904.6	$133,857.4
Sample Totals	16,064.7	24,710.1	28,098.0	23,297.1	27,319.8	62,306.1	64,959.9
Sample Cities							
Gary, Ind.	148.1	403.5	403.5	407.4	437.7	736.0	786.6
Long Beach, Ca.	690.0	934.1	974.2	853.2	1,015.0	2,213.9	2,286.9
New York, N.Y.	11,171.0	17,495.7	19,540.2	16,347.7	18,873.0	45,835.9	47,844.7
Philadelphia, Pa.	3,658.7	5,023.9	6,327.2	4,942.3	6,247.6	11,920.0	12,402.0
St. Paul, Minn.	294.4	718.1	718.1	628.5	628.5	1,301.8	1,301.8
Topeka, Kansas	102.5	134.8	134.8	118.0	118.0	298.5	337.9
Sample Counties	3,728.0	3,991.1	4,713.1	3,618.0	4,639.6	11,714.6	12,568.2
Calhoun, Mich.	167.2	425.0	509.5	374.9	421.4	728.0	799.7
Chester, Pa.	101.2	-0-	-0-	-0-	-0-	411.3	411.3
Bal. of Cook, Ill.	848.6	664.4	664.4	676.8	941.6	3,777.9	3,777.9
Lorain, Ohio	133.0	173.4	173.4	151.7	151.7	490.9	697.9
Middlesex, N.J.	797.5	1,217.8	1,217.8	1,224.6	1,420.4	3,294.1	3,531.7
Pasco, Fla.	171.5	222.3	222.3	-0-	-0-	353.3	382.7
Bal. of Ramsey, Minn.	71.4	-0-	-0-	-0-	-0-	253.5	253.5
Stanislaus, Ca.	1,246.6	1,067.1	1,704.6	970.4	1,459.5	1,492.0	1,686.4
Bal. of Union, N.J.	101.0	221.1					

Sample Consortia	5,664.4	7,594.5	8,859.9	6,950.4	8,258.8	24,749.7	26,787.0
Austin, Texas	100.3	-0-	-0-	-0-	-0-	490.6	490.6
Cleveland, Ohio	(1,738.4)	2,756.2	3,321.1	2,628.1	3,220.8	7,139.1	7,608.6
Kansas City, Kansas	(124.3)	89.2	89.2	78.1	78.1	448.5	523.1
Lansing, Mich.	183.7	1,258.0	1,451.9	1,098.0	1,367.6	1,440.4	1,647.8
Phoenix/Maricopa, Ariz.	724.6	585.9	763.3	617.4	792.7	5,323.2	5,710.8
Orange County, Ca.	1,503.9	1,769.8	1,769.8	1,608.9	1,637.1	6,727.5	7,126.0
Raleigh, N.C.	(106.7)	-0-	-0-	-0-	-0-	687.0	771.0
St. Petersburg, Fla.	153.7	118.3	118.3	32.2	32.2	1,343.5	1,507.8
San Joaquin, Ca.	1,028.8	1,017.1	1,346.3	887.7	1,130.3	1,149.9	1,401.3[2]
Sample States	2,072.9	3,234.1	3,825.6	3,189.2	3,810.9	23,134.2	29,542.3
Maine	1,500.0	2,467.8	2,771.1	2,208.3	2,675.1	3,867.3	4,797.6[2]
Bal. of Arizona	572.9	140.5	140.5	340.5	400.5	1,736.2	1,812.6
Bal. of North Carolina	NA	-0-	-0-	98.7	98.7	11,087.0	14,091.7
Bal. of Texas	NA	625.8	914.0	541.7	636.6	6,443.7	8,840.4

Source: Manpower Administration, U.S. Department of Labor
[1] The totals include the formula allocation plus allotments to prime sponsors from the discretionary fund.
[2] Title VI discretionary allotment includes an adjustment to provide 90% of original planning estimate issued by the Department of Labor.
( ) Estimated.
(Details may not add to totals due to rounding.)

TABLE 4 CETA Title I Allocations, Fiscal Year 1975, Sample Prime Sponsors (amounts in thousands)

Prime Sponsor	FY 1974 Allocation Base	FY 1975 Formula Allocation	Percent of 1974 Allocation Base	FY 1975 Adjusted Allocation[1]	Percent of 1974 Allocation Base	Total FY 1975 Allocation[2]
	(1)	(2)	(3)	(4)	(5)	(6)
National Totals	$1,406,647.5	$1,249,360.0	88.8	$1,353,718.9	96.2	$1,392,290.9
Sample Totals	213,054.8	184,176.2	86.5	200,635.5	94.2	204,633.5
Sample Cities	97,886.2	79,943.6	81.2	88,097.6	90.0	88,097.6
Gary	5,625.7	2,985.5	53.1	5,063.1	90.0	5,063.1
Long Beach	3,025.1	2,644.0	87.4	2,722.6	90.0	2,722.6
New York	70,074.4	57,251.2	81.7	63,067.0	90.0	63,067.4
Philadelphia	15,479.6	13,706.6	88.6	13,931.6	90.0	13,931.6
St. Paul	2,597.9	2,111.9	81.3	2,338.1	90.0	2,338.1
Topeka	1,083.5	794.4	73.3	975.2	90.0	975.2
Sample Counties	13,092.8	16,897.4	129.1	16,749.7	127.9	16,749.7
Calhoun, Mich.	849.3	853.7	100.5	853.7	100.5	853.7
Chester, Pa.	1,052.6	1,028.4	97.7	1,028.4	97.7	1,028.4
Bal. of Cook Co., Ill.	4,823.3	6,665.6	138.2	6,665.6	138.2	6,665.6
Lorain, Ohio	648.0	841.2	129.8	841.2	129.8	841.2
Middlesex, N.J.	2,468.0	2,947.5	119.4	2,947.5	119.4	2,947.5
Pasco, Fla.	253.6	502.9	198.3	380.4	150.0	380.4
Bal. of Ramsey, Minn.	313.7	495.5	158.0	470.6	150.0	470.6
Stanislaus, Calif.	1,346.1	1,972.4	146.5	1,972.4	146.5	1,972.4
Bal. of Union, N.J.	1,338.2	1,590.2	118.8	1,590.2	118.8	1,590.2

152

Sample Consortia	42,139.0	36,457.0	86.5	41,662.1	98.9	45,660.1
Austin, Texas	2,669.8	2,203.8	82.6	2,467.6	92.4	2,714.4
Cleveland, Ohio	15,031.1	11,274.4	75.0	14,164.5	94.2	15,581.0
Kansas City, Kansas	1,804.3	1,306.3	72.4	1,623.9	90.0	1,623.9
Lansing, Mich.	1,917.9	1,810.0	94.4	1,979.8	103.2	2,177.8
Phoenix/Maricopa, Ariz.	8,279.4	6,370.6	77.0	7,451.5	90.0	8,196.6
Orange County, Calif.	5,648.7	6,905.9	122.3	7,029.5	124.4	7,732.5
Raleigh, N.C.	2,075.6	1,791.8	86.3	2,031.8	97.9	2,235.0
St. Petersburg, Fla.	2,194.3	2,291.8	104.4	2,291.8	104.4	2,521.0
San Joaquin, Calif.	2,517.9	2,502.4	99.4	2,621.7	104.1	2,883.9
Sample States	59,936.8	50,878.2	84.9	54,126.1	90.3	54,126.1
Maine	7,879.0	7,052.8	89.5	7,091.1	90.0	7,091.1[3]
Bal. of Arizona	5,735.5	4,034.5	70.3	5,162.0	90.0	5,162.0
Bal. of North Carolina	24,524.4	20,769.3	84.7	22,108.7	90.2	22,108.7
Bal. of Texas	21,797.9	19,021.6	87.3	19,764.3	90.7	19,764.3

Source: Manpower Administration, U.S. Department of Labor

[1] Adjusted to a minimum of 90 percent of prior year's allocation or a maximum of 150 percent.

[2] This column excludes State Manpower Services and Vocational Educations funds. Consortium incentive funds are included for all consortia except Kansas City, which did not qualify.

[3] The figure for Maine excludes:

$ 71,240 1% State Manpower Services Council
  445,253 5% Supplemental Vocational Education Services
  356,202 4% State Services
—————
$872,695

(Details may not add to totals due to rounding.)

TABLE 5 CETA Title I Allocations, Fiscal Year 1975, Compared with Obligations for Comparable Manpower Programs for Fiscal Year 1974, by State (amounts in thousands)

State	FY 1974				FY 1975			
	New Obligations	Percent Dist.	Manpower Allocations[1]	Percent Dist.	Title I Formula Amount[2]	Percent Dist.	Title I Allocations[2]	Percent Dist.
	(1)	(2)	(3)	(4)	(5)	(6)	(7)	(8)
U.S. Total	$1,160,653	100.0	$1,406,648	100.0	$1,249,360	100.0	$1,353,717	100.0
Alabama	21,718	1.9	26,819	1.9	21,848	1.8	24,538	1.8
Arizona	16,069	1.4	16,457	1.2	12,346	1.0	14,812	1.1
Arkansas	13,252	1.1	16,995	1.2	13,787	1.1	15,404	1.1
California	115,016	9.9	131,837	9.4	135,093	10.8	137,712	10.2
Colorado	9,479	.8	12,983	.9	11,119	.9	12,160	.9
Connecticut	18,601	1.6	21,351	1.5	18,903	1.5	21,257	1.6
Delaware	2,754	.2	3,450	.3	3,084	.3	3,461	.3
District of Columbia	13,648	1.2	17,213	1.2	10,466	.8	15,492	1.1
Florida	35,217	3.0	40,931	2.9	38,853	3.1	40,362	3.0
Georgia	25,651	2.2	30,896	2.2	26,826	2.2	28,213	2.1
Idaho	3,978	.3	5,145	.4	4,905	.4	4,998	.4
Illinois	57,180	4.9	72,453	5.2	59,574	4.8	70,203	5.2
Indiana	24,014	2.1	30,545	2.2	27,182	2.2	30,913	2.3
Iowa	12,674	1.1	14,794	1.1	12,747	1.0	13,868	1.0
Kansas	8,243	.7	11,869	.8	10,552	.8	11,256	.8
Kentucky	25,473	2.2	27,931	2.0	22,345	1.8	25,390	1.9
Louisiana	25,183	2.2	30,140	2.1	26,135	2.1	27,256	2.0
Maine	6,558	.6	7,879	.6	7,053	.6	7,091	.5
Maryland	19,182	1.7	22,855	1.6	18,644	1.5	21,593	1.6
Massachusetts	31,724	2.7	39,381	2.8	38,423	3.1	40,863	3.0
Michigan	41,616	3.6	56,922	4.1	53,106	4.3	55,908	4.1
Minnesota	20,465	1.8	23,512	1.7	21,286	1.7	22,331	1.7
Mississippi	17,650	1.5	21,587	1.5	16,073	1.3	19,428	1.4

State							
Missouri	25,220	2.2	32,910	2.3	26,360	2.1	30,878	2.3
Montana	4,306	.4	4,678	.3	4,735	.4	4,735	.4
Nebraska	8,484	.7	9,479	.7	7,913	.6	8,613	.6
Nevada	3,650	.3	4,231	.3	3,847	.3	4,047	.3
New Hampshire	4,258	.4	4,202	.3	3,677	.3	3,963	.3
New Jersey	39,082	3.4	46,799	3.3	43,120	3.5	48,280	3.6
New Mexico	10,999	1.0	10,201	.7	8,018	.6	9,181	.7
New York	108,154	9.3	124,303	8.8	109,102	8.7	117,099	8.7
North Carolina	30,199	2.6	36,544	2.6	30,387	2.4	33,221	2.5
North Dakota	3,225	.3	4,060	.3	3,821	.3	3,821	.3
Ohio	42,859	3.7	60,408	4.3	53,811	4.3	60,285	4.3
Oklahoma	19,465	1.7	18,347	1.3	15,903	1.3	16,728	1.2
Oregon	10,834	.9	14,009	1.0	13,283	1.1	13,977	1.0
Pennsylvania	54,737	4.7	68,982	4.9	64,293	5.2	67,880	5.0
Rhode Island	5,651	.5	6,925	.5	6,440	.5	7,394	.6
South Carolina	19,113	1.7	20,444	1.5	16,404	1.3	18,512	1.4
South Dakota	3,883	.3	4,210	.3	3,621	.3	3,789	.3
Tennessee	24,195	2.1	29,371	2.1	23,676	1.9	26,434	2.0
Texas	61,561	5.3	75,044	5.3	64,165	5.1	69,382	5.1
Utah	5,534	.5	7,042	.5	6,655	.5	6,666	.5
Vermont	2,561	.2	3,274	.2	2,962	.2	2,962	.2
Virginia	20,017	1.7	28,005	2.0	24,210	1.9	26,059	1.9
Washington	22,614	2.0	27,563	2.0	26,201	2.1	27,029	2.0
West Virginia	12,014	1.0	14,671	1.0	12,708	1.0	13,291	1.0
Wisconsin	22,105	1.9	24,524	1.7	22,420	1.8	23,059	1.7
Wyoming	1,485	.2	2,131	.2	1,756	.1	1,918	.1
Alaska, Hawaii, & Puerto Rico	29,103	2.5	40,350	2.9	39,344	3.2	40,012	3.0

Source: Manpower Administration

[1] FY 1974 obligations used as base for FY 1975 Title I allocations. Includes Summer Youth program funds.

[2] Excludes allotments for territories and rural CEP's. Also excludes funds for State Manpower Services Councils, supplemental vocational education, State manpower services, and consortium incentives.

(Details may not add to totals due to rounding.)

TABLE 6 Federal Obligations for Manpower Programs, Total and Department of Labor, Compared with Gross National Product Fiscal Years 1972-1976 (amounts in millions of dollars)

| Fiscal Year | Obligations for Manpower Programs | | | Gross National Product (GNP) | Total Obligations as Percent of GNP |
| | Total All Agencies | Department of Labor | | | |
		Amount	Percent of Total		
	(1)	(2)	(3)	(4)	(5)
1972	4,941	3,348	67.8	1,102,000	0.45
1973	5,252	3,432	65.3	1,224,000	0.43
1974	4,641	2,817	60.7	1,349,000	0.34
1975 (est.)	6,827	4,590	67.2	1,434,000	0.48
1976 (est.)	5,411	3,274	60.5	1,596,000	0.34

Source: Cols. 1 and 2, Office of Management and Budget, Special Analyses, Budget of the United States, Fiscal Year 1975 and Fiscal Year 1976.

TABLE 7 Federal Obligations and Participants, Manpower Programs Corresponding with CETA Title I, Fiscal Year 1974

Program	With Summer Youth Employment				Without Summer Youth Employment			
	Obligations		Participants		Obligations		Participants	
	$000	Percent	Number	Percent	$000	Percent	Number	Percent
	(1)	(2)	(3)	(4)	(5)	(6)	(7)	(8)
Total	1,402,438	100	1,384,900	100	942,947	100	796,100	100
Classroom Training	377,986	27	254,800	18	377,986	40	254,800	32
MDTA Institutional	283,812		152,800		283,812		152,800	
MDTA Section 241	5,488		NA		5,488		NA	
OIC	23,251		28,000		23,251		28,000	
SER	12,097		6,400		12,097		6,400	
CEP/CMP[1]	53,338		67,600		53,338		67,600	
On-the-Job Training	182,828	13	149,800	11	182,828	20	149,800	19
MDTA JOPS	49,937		52,500		49,937		52,500	
MDTA Section 241	401		NA		401		NA	
JOBS	64,026		42,200		64,026		42,200	
Urban League	7,796		6,600		7,796		6,600	
Public Service Careers	28,334		29,700		28,334		29,700	
Hometown Plans	3,454		NA		3,454		NA	
CEP/CMP[1]	28,880		18,800		28,880		18,800	
Work Experience	820,375	58	980,300	71	360,884	38	391,500	49
NYC In-School	88,570		163,400		88,570		163,400	
NYC Out-of-School	113,651		105,800		113,651		105,800	
Operation Mainstream	94,879		66,800		94,879		66,800	
CEP/CMP[1]	63,784		55,500		63,784		55,500	
Summer Youth	459,491		588,800		—		—	
Other	21,249	2	—		21,249	2	—	
CAMPS/GOV 5% Fund; other	21,249		—		21,249		—	

Source: Computed from Manpower Administration figures.

[1] Obligations and participants for the Concentrated Employment Programs and Comprehensive Manpower Programs were prorated among activities.

TABLE 8 Planned and Actual Expenditures by Program Activity, CETA Title I, Fiscal Year 1975, Sample Prime Sponsors

Prime Sponsors		Accrued Expenditures FY 1975 ($000)	Classroom Training		On-the-Job Training	Public Service Employment	Work Experience	Services to Clients and Other Activities
			Prime Sponsor	Vocational Education[1]				
		(1)	(2)	(3)	(4)	(5)	(6)	(7)
CITIES								
Gary	Planned	4,252.0	38.8	0.7	15.5	1.6	35.3	8.1
	Actual	2,775.5	45.3	–	6.9	2.3	36.9	8.6
	% of Plan	65.3						
Long Beach	Planned	1,406.0	36.1	11.1	17.8	–	20.8	14.2
	Actual	1,257.0	44.7	11.8	13.2	–	15.6	14.7
	% of Plan	89.4						
New York	Planned	40,211.0	36.8	–	21.6	–	38.6	3.0
	Actual	32,143.0	39.6	–	18.5	–	39.2	2.7
	% of Plan	79.9						
Philadelphia	Planned	10,311.0	45.9	4.4	8.0	2.1	29.4	10.3
	Actual	10,422.0	43.5	5.0	8.1	0.2	30.2	13.1
	% of Plan	101.1						
St. Paul	Planned	NA	NA	NA	NA	NA	NA	NA
	Actual	1,067.8	14.8	7.1	6.3	–	7.4	64.5
	% of Plan	NA						
Topeka	Planned	777.0	34.1	–	10.3	–	30.9	24.7
	Actual	716.0	51.7	–	2.4	–	34.2	11.7
	% of Plan	92.2						
COUNTIES								
Calhoun	Planned	733.0	28.1	5.6	7.0	–	42.0	17.3
	Actual	75.6	41.0	–	–	–	–	59.0
	% of Plan	10.3						

158

Chester	Planned	772.0	10.6	0.8	3.4	—	66.6	2.6
	Actual	688.1	15.9	1.5	0.7	—	80.9	1.0
	% of Plan	89.1						
Cook	Planned	2,776.0	27.4	13.3	7.7	17.8	33.9	—
	Actual	2,534.6	26.7	13.7	9.4	14.4	35.8	—
	% of Plan	91.3						
Lorain	Planned	745.0	36.1	6.7	1.7	14.9	6.9	33.7
	Actual	565.6	40.1	4.3	2.2	21.1	3.5	28.9
	% of Plan	75.9						
Middlesex	Planned	1,732.0	49.1	2.5	10.5	—	22.2	15.8
	Actual	1,632.0	43.4	3.0	10.4	—	26.6	18.2
	% of Plan	94.2						
Pasco	Planned	355.0	7.0	5.6	7.0	—	58.3	22.0
	Actual	264.1	6.1	5.5	0.5	—	56.6	31.3
	% of Plan	74.4						
Ramsey	Planned	525.0	32.4	6.3	5.5	—	42.9	13.0
	Actual	330.2	26.7	4.1	2.2	—	55.3	11.7
	% of Plan	62.9						
Stanislaus	Planned	1,065.0	12.2	1.9	48.8	—	37.1	—
	Actual	906.1	18.8	—	32.0	—	49.2	—
	% of Plan	85.1						
Union	Planned	939.0	22.8	—	16.0	—	32.7	28.5
	Actual	544.0	40.6	14.3	2.8	2.4	31.6	8.3
	% of Plan	57.9						

TABLE 8 (Continued)

Prime Sponsors		Accrued Expenditures FY 1975 ($000)	Percent Distribution by Program Activity					
			Classroom Training		On-the-Job Training	Public Service Employment	Work Experience	Services to Clients and Other Activities
			Prime Sponsor	Vocational Education[1]				
		(1)	(2)	(3)	(4)	(5)	(6)	(7)
CONSORTIA								
Austin	Planned	2,980.0	41.6	4.8	9.9	—	43.8	—
	Actual	2,586.4	30.9	3.1	10.0	—	56.0	—
	% of Plan	86.8						
Cleveland	Planned	11,440.0	24.0	6.9	5.8	32.7	21.1	9.6
	Actual	10,424.3	22.7	—	4.0	35.3	20.3	17.8
	% of Plan	91.1						
Kansas City	Planned	NA	NA	NA	NA	NA	NA	NA
	Actual	NA	NA	NA	NA	NA	NA	NA
	% of Plan	NA						
Lansing	Planned	1,419.0	9.2	—	10.7	—	61.1	19.0
	Actual	1,267.3	6.7	1.6	12.3	—	67.0	12.5
	% of Plan	89.3						
Phoenix/Maricopa	Planned	1,682.0	26.2	4.9	13.1	0.5	33.6	21.7
	Actual	1,456.0	14.4	5.7	6.0	0.7	35.2	38.1
	% of Plan	86.6						
Orange	Planned	4,561.0	33.1	—	7.7	0.7	52.8	5.7
	Actual	3,844.2	33.6	—	9.9	1.1	49.7	5.7
	% of Plan	84.3						
Raleigh	Planned	2,118.0	40.3	4.1	1.1	—	43.0	11.5
	Actual	1,471.4	46.0	—	1.2	—	40.8	12.0
	% of Plan	69.5						
Pinellas/St. Petersburg	Planned	2,305.0	22.3	3.0	2.7	—	56.0	16.0
	Actual	2,230.7	23.7	2.9	2.3	—	54.6	16.6
	% of Plan	96.8						

San Joaquin	Planned	1,505.0	19.3	—	7.0	—	40.6	33.1
	Actual	2,071.9	12.8	—	12.1	—	61.4	13.7
	% of Plan	137.6						
STATES								
Maine	Planned	7,066.0	18.4	—	17.2	—	63.8	0.7
	Actual	6,237.0	18.1	—	12.7	—	68.7	0.5
	% of Plan	89.0						
Bal. of Arizona	Planned	3,212.0	26.7	—	6.2	32.4	25.8	8.9
	Actual	2,766.9	28.1	—	3.5	28.4	31.9	8.1
	% of Plan	86.1						
Bal. of N. Carolina	Planned	19,755.0	23.6	5.2	5.5	3.3	62.2	0.2
	Actual	19,551.9	20.3	7.7	3.5	1.9	66.7	—
	% of Plan	99.0						
Bal. of Texas	Planned	22,726.0	17.6	4.3	4.4	8.8	64.9	—
	Actual	14,739.7	14.3	—	5.1	8.9	59.6	12.2
	% of Plan	64.9						

Source: Quarterly Progress Reports, Manpower Administration, U.S. Department of Labor
[1] Classroom training supported with the States' 5% supplemental Vocational Education funds.
(Details may not add to 100 percent due to rounding.)

TABLE 9 Planned and Actual Enrollees by Program Activity, CETA Title I, Fiscal Year 1975, Sample Prime Sponsors

	Total Enrollees[1] (Cumulative)	Percent Distribution by Program Activity					
		Classroom Training		On-the-Job Training	Public Service Employment	Work Experience	Other
Prime Sponsors		Prime Sponsor	Vocational Education[2]				
	(1)	(2)	(3)	(4)	(5)	(6)	(7)
CITIES							
Gary							
Planned	3,238	19.7	1.1	7.0	0.5	71.7	—
Actual	1,704	42.6	—	6.0	0.8	50.5	—
% of Plan	52.6						
Long Beach							
Planned	3,351	52.9	9.4	15.6	—	22.1	—
Actual	3,068	34.7	10.3	6.9	—	14.9	33.2
% of Plan	91.6						
New York							
Planned	21,113	28.7	—	19.5	—	15.4	36.5
Actual	25,163	23.8	—	12.2	—	32.7	31.3
% of Plan	119.2						
Philadelphia							
Planned	9,900	57.4	7.2	5.7	1.6	23.1	5.0
Actual	10,163	62.3	7.2	5.6	0.4	20.6	4.0
% of Plan	102.7						
St. Paul							
Planned	1,292	31.9	5.3	15.5	—	4.8	42.5
Actual	1,358	32.6	1.2	12.7	—	7.4	46.2
% of Plan	105.1						
Topeka							
Planned	782	44.8	12.2	8.3	—	33.5	1.3
Actual	840	59.1	—	3.9	—	35.6	1.4
% of Plan	107.4						

COUNTIES								
Calhoun	Planned	428	28.0	7.2	8.4	—	56.3	—
	Actual	129	—	100.0	—	—	—	—
	% of Plan	30.1						
Chester	Planned	820	22.0	8.8	6.7	—	62.6	—
	Actual	956	14.6	13.6	1.1	—	70.7	—
	% of Plan	116.6						
Cook	Planned	3,351	14.9	—	2.7	10.9	71.5	—
	Actual	3,068	18.9	—	2.3	12.7	66.0	—
	% of Plan	91.6						
Lorain	Planned	781	38.2	28.3	9.6	3.3	20.6	—
	Actual	793	53.3	9.0	6.9	3.9	26.9	—
	% of Plan	101.5						
Middlesex	Planned	1,052	39.2	9.0	8.8	—	43.0	—
	Actual	1,018	31.2	9.2	12.1	—	47.5	—
	% of Plan	96.8						
Pasco	Planned	556	18.2	—	34.5	—	47.3	—
	Actual	394	32.7	—	0.5	—	66.8	—
	% of Plan	70.9						
Ramsey	Planned	335	16.4	19.1	4.5	—	60.0	—
	Actual	619	13.7	13.7	2.4	—	70.1	—
	% of Plan	184.8						
Stanislaus	Planned	1,248	9.6	—	24.0	—	60.1	6.3
	Actual	1,565	9.8	—	30.4	—	59.7	—
	% of Plan	125.4						
Union	Planned	570	52.6	—	19.3	—	28.1	—
	Actual	719	50.6	0.8	1.7	—	46.9	—
	% of Plan	126.1						

TABLE 9 (Continued)

Prime Sponsors		Total Enrollees[1] (Cumulative)	Percent Distribution by Program Activity					
			Classroom Training		On-the-Job Training	Public Service Employment	Work Experience	Other
			Prime Sponsor	Vocational Education[2]				
		(1)	(2)	(3)	(4)	(5)	(6)	(7)
CONSORTIA								
Austin	Planned	2,137	6.3	23.4	10.0	—	60.3	—
	Actual	1,974	2.4	28.3	6.4	—	62.9	‥
	% of Plan	92.4						
Cleveland	Planned	10,207	19.2	4.7	3.0	7.6	53.3	12.2
	Actual	5,449	27.5	0.5	3.3	11.5	55.6	1.7
	% of Plan	53.4						
Kansas City	Planned	2,077	68.4	7.1	3.4	—	20.9	0.2
	Actual	2,211	82.0	2.1	2.5	‥	11.9	1.5
	% of Plan	106.5						
Lansing	Planned	4,628	1.9	—	2.3	—	37.7	58.2
	Actual	4,929	2.3	1.4	2.3	—	35.8	58.2
	% of Plan	106.5						
Phoenix/Maricopa	Planned	5,253	44.8	1.4	7.4	0.1	45.0	1.3
	Actual	3,810	41.0	2.7	9.1	0.8	45.7	0.8
	% of Plan	72.5						
Orange	Planned	6,407	24.2	6.5	3.9	0.2	65.2	—
	Actual	6,593	20.1	6.1	4.5	0.2	69.1	—
	% of Plan	102.9						
Raleigh	Planned	1,309	28.4	1.3	1.8	—	68.5	—
	Actual	1,585	22.7	—	1.3	—	76.0	—
	% of Plan	121.1						
Pinellas/St. Petersburg	Planned	2,066	33.4	9.0	11.6	—	46.0	—
	Actual	1,964	29.8	9.7	6.9	—	53.5	—
	% of Plan	95.1						

		Total Enrollees[1]						
San Joaquin	Planned	1,267	36.7	—	5.7	—	57.6	—
	Actual	3,223	14.1	—	4.5	—	81.5	—
	% of Plan	254.4						
STATES								
Maine	Planned	4,402	14.2	—	20.3	—	65.5	—
	Actual	5,516	13.7	—	19.1	—	67.2	—
	% of Plan	125.3						
Bal. of Arizona	Planned	2,560	20.8	5.4	10.0	11.9	47.0	4.9
	Actual	2,316	25.1	—	4.1	17.1	53.8	—
	% of Plan	90.5						
Bal. of N. Carolina	Planned	17,641	10.7	15.2	6.8	1.0	66.4	—
	Actual	15,692	10.1	10.4	7.5	1.9	70.1	—
	% of Plan	89.0						
Bal. of Texas	Planned	17,055	7.0	5.3	4.1	2.4	81.2	—
	Actual	16,586	12.0	5.5	5.8	3.3	71.7	1.8
	% of Plan	97.3						

Source: Quarterly Progress Reports, Manpower Administration, U.S. Department of Labor
[1] "Total Enrollees" measures persons enrolled in program activities. An individual may be counted more than once if enrolled in more than one activity. Participants are not counted if they receive services but are not enrolled in a program activity.
[2] Classroom training supported with the States 5% supplemental Vocational Education funds.
(Details may not add to 100 percent due to rounding.)

TABLE 10 Characteristics of Participants in CETA Title I, Fiscal Year 1975, Sample Prime Sponsors

							Percent of Total				
Prime Sponsors	Participants[1] (Cumulative)	Female	Age 21 and Under	Age 45 and Over	8 Years or Less of School	12 Years or More of School	Economically Disadvantaged	White	Black	Spanish Speaking	Veterans
	(1)	(2)	(3)	(4)	(5)	(6)	(7)	(8)	(9)	(10)	(11)
CITIES											
Gary	1,664	51.2	50.8	4.3	11.3	43.9	99.1	14.4	85.0	10.8	5.8
Long Beach	1,700	43.8	46.4	5.4	4.5	51.6	98.6	40.2	37.6	12.9	5.5
New York	25,163	48.8	56.9	7.0	9.6	38.3	76.5	29.5	62.5	21.8	12.8
Philadelphia	10,857	46.3	54.5	3.3	6.8	47.9	77.6	9.6	85.8	6.0	6.9
St. Paul	3,900	39.5	39.3	10.5	3.1	67.5	64.7	76.6	17.8	2.5	15.1
Topeka	712	51.0	61.5	2.0	3.8	43.3	82.6	42.1	44.2	11.2	11.7
COUNTIES											
Calhoun	129	43.4	48.1	3.1	0.8	71.3	74.4	30.5	63.6	8.5	12.4
Chester	953	52.4	70.2	4.4	19.1	23.9	61.8	51.2	47.4	21.0	3.2
Cook	3,068	48.5	67.2	15.0	8.7	28.0	51.6	40.1	59.5	8.5	6.9
Lorain	784	41.8	65.3	13.0	8.8	52.4	56.3	44.8	38.4	16.7	8.6
Middlesex	1,369	50.2	61.8	2.3	15.1	33.0	66.5	26.5	49.8	15.9	5.1
Pasco	1,476	45.1	37.0	15.9	12.5	50.8	58.5	79.0	16.4	4.2	17.9
Ramsey	692	48.3	69.3	1.5	13.2	46.2	85.7	94.9	2.0	1.3	7.4
Stanislaus	1,565	39.9	71.2	8.4	6.1	31.7	53.4	89.8	6.5	22.6	10.4
Union	NA	NA	NA	NA	NA	NA	NA	NA	NA	NA	NA

CONSORTIA

Austin	1,790	56.8	61.8	4.1	14.5	30.4	92.0	64.6	35.3	39.9	4.7
Cleveland	6,838	48.3	57.4	13.3	11.4	35.0	74.1	41.2	58.5	13.5	10.5
Kansas City	1,980	51.3	52.9	4.2	6.2	52.9	70.8	36.0	52.6	1.9	13.0
Lansing	4,929	39.7	50.8	6.6	10.9	46.7	68.9	58.6	36.6	13.3	8.8
Phoenix/Maricopa	4,377	51.9	58.8	2.5	14.6	32.9	93.2	67.6	27.5	43.1	8.0
Orange	6,859	46.7	71.5	5.1	7.2	34.4	95.2	84.5	9.5	46.9	7.7
Raleigh	1,525	46.0	66.3	3.8	17.3	30.9	52.7	26.4	73.3	0.0	1.7
St. Petersburg	3,250	45.6	44.7	7.7	7.8	46.9	79.6	50.4	49.0	0.1	10.6
San Joaquin	5,930	40.6	61.7	9.7	17.4	35.8	74.5	66.0	22.6	42.9	4.8

STATES

Maine	5,516	36.7	44.2	8.0	11.2	52.2	86.7	97.3	0.6	0.1	19.2
Bal. of Arizona	2,175	43.0	52.2	7.0	17.6	39.8	77.8	42.4	4.0	18.7	9.3
Bal. of N. Carolina	15,692	48.0	65.9	3.5	21.0	24.1	82.0	43.7	54.6	0.1	9.4
Bal. of Texas	15,576	44.9	73.9	5.3	18.1	21.5	84.9	64.7	34.9	32.3	4.5

Source: Quarterly Summary of Client Characteristics, Manpower Administration, U.S. Department of Labor
[1] Non-duplicative sum of persons enrolled in program activities plus those receiving non-program services (child-care, direct placement, etc.).

TABLE 11 Characteristics of Participants in CETA Titles I, II, and VI Programs, Fiscal Year 1975, Compared With Participants in Similar Fiscal Year 1974 Programs

Characteristics	CETA Title I	Categorical Programs FY 1974[1]	CETA Title II	CETA Title VI	PEP 1974
	(1)	(2)	(3)	(4)	(5)
Total: Number	1,034,500[2]	549,700	200,100	141,100	66,200[3]
Percent	100.0	100.0	100.0	100.0	100.0
Male	54.4	57.7	65.8	70.2	66.1
Female	45.6	42.3	34.2	29.8	33.9
Age: Under 22	61.7	63.1	23.7	21.4	22.8
22–44	32.1	30.5	62.9	64.8	66.5
45–54	3.5	6.2	8.4	9.1	
55 and over	2.6		5.0	4.7	10.7
Education: 8 grades or less	13.3	15.1	9.4	8.4	
9–11	47.6	51.1	18.3	18.2	22.9
12 and over	39.1	33.6	72.3	73.3	77.2
On Public Assistance: AFDC	15.5	23.4	6.6	5.6	
Other	11.3		9.2	8.1	10.1
Economically disadvantaged	77.3	86.7	48.3	43.6	34.1
Race: White	54.6	54.9	65.1	71.1	68.8
Black	38.5	37.0	21.8	22.9	22.9
American Indian	1.3	3.5	1.0	1.1	3.3
Other	5.6[4]	4.6	12.1[4]	9.5[4]	5.0
Spanish American	12.5	15.4	9.6	11.8	13.2
Limited English-speaking ability	4.1	NA	8.0	4.6	NA
Migrants or seasonal farm workers	1.6	NA	1.0	1.0	NA

168

Veteran: Special Vietnam	5.2	15.3	11.3	12.5	39.2
Other	4.4		12.6	14.6	
Handicapped	3.8	6.3	3.2	2.9	4.2
Full-time student	32.8	NA	3.0	2.8	NA
Offender	5.7	NA	2.9	2.6	NA
Labor Force Status:					
Employed	2.3	7.6[5]	3.9	2.0	NA
Underemployed	4.5	8.7[5]	8.4	6.4	9.7
Unemployed	61.6	75.6[5]	83.6	88.4	90.3
Not in labor force	31.6	8.1[5]	4.1	3.1	NA
Receiving unemployment insurance	3.9	4.6	12.0	14.6	7.4
Median hourly wage of employed terminees					
Pre-enrollment	$2.60	$2.30	$2.87	$3.02	2.78
Post-enrollment	$2.76	$2.86[6]	$3.36	$3.57	NA

Source: Manpower Administration, U.S. Department of Labor
[1] Includes MDTA-Institutional, JOP–OJT, NYC In-school, NYC Out-of-School, Operation Mainstream, CEP and JOBS.
[2] Preliminary data.
[3] Excludes enrollees in PEP summer youth program for whom data were not available.
[4] A large portion of participants falling into this group reflect the non-classification by ethnic categories in Puerto Rico.
[5] Excludes NYC In-school and JOBS enrollees for whom data was not available.
[6] Includes MDTA-Institutional, OJT, CEP, JOP.
ı NA = Information Not Available
(Details may not add to 100 percent due to rounding.)

Bibliography

Aronson, Robert L. ed. The Localization of Federal Manpower Planning. Ithaca: New York State School of Industrial and Labor Relations, 1973.

"Building a Manpower Partnership." Manpower, 6(4): 10-15, 1974.

Committee on Evaluation of Employment and Training Programs. "Early Perceptions of the Comprehensive Employment and Training Act." Washington, D. C.: National Academy of Sciences, 1974.

Comprehensive Employment and Training Act of 1973. PL 93-203. Statutes at Large 87, sec. 839, 1974.

Davidson, Roger H. The Politics of Comprehensive Manpower Legislation. Policy Studies in Employment and Welfare, no. 15. Baltimore: Johns Hopkins Press, 1972.

Emergency Jobs and Unemployment Assistance Act of 1974. PL 93-567. Statutes at Large 88, sec. 1845, 1974.

Guttman, Robert, "Intergovernmental Relations Under the New Manpower Act." Monthly Labor Review, 97(6): 10-16, 1974.

Kobrak, Peter and E. Earl Wright. "CETA: The View
from Kalamazoo." In J. L. Stern and Barbara D.
Dennis, eds. Proceedings of the Twenty-Seventh
Annual Winter Meeting. San Francisco: Industrial
Relations Research Association, 1974.

Kolberg, William H. "CETA Progress Report."
Manpower, 6(11):9-12, 1974.

Levitan, Sar A. and Garth L. Mangum. Federal Training and Work Programs in the Sixties. Ann Arbor:
Institute of Labor and Industrial Relations, University
of Michigan and Wayne State University, 1969.

Mangum, Garth L. and David Snedeker. Manpower
Planning for Local Labor Markets. Salt Lake City:
Olympus Publishing Company, 1974.

Mirengoff, William. Manpower Programs under CETA;
A Preliminary Assessment." unpublished paper.
Washington, D. C., National Academy of Sciences, 1975.

National League of Cities/U. S. Conference of Mayors.
"The Impact of CETA on Institutional Vocation Educa-
tion." Washington, D. C.: National League of Cities/
U. S. Conference of Mayors, 1974.

National Manpower Policy Task Force. The Comprehensive Employment and Training Act: Opportunities
and Challenges. Washington, D. C.: National Manpower Policy Task Force, 1974.

Ruttenberg, Stanley H. assisted by Jocelyn Gutchess.
Manpower Challenge of the 1970's: Institutions and
Social Change. Policy Studies in Employment and Wel-
fare, no. 2. Baltimore: Johns Hopkins Press, 1972.

Southern Regional Council. "The Job Ahead: Manpower
Policies in the South." Atlanta: Southern Regional
Council, 1975.

U. S. Congress. Conference Report on S. 1559, the Comprehensive Employment and Training Act of 1973. 93d Cong., 1st sess. Washington, D. C.: U. S. Government Printing Office, 1973.

U. S. Congress. House. Committee on Education and Labor. Hearings on H. R. 11010 and H. R. 11011 to Assure Opportunities for Employment and Training to Unemployed and Underemployed Persons. Hearings before the Select Subcommittee on Labor, 93d Cong., 1st sess. Washington, D. C.: U. S. Government Printing Office, 1973.

U. S. Congress. House. Committee on Education and Labor. Report on H. R. 11010, The Comprehensive Manpower Act of 1973. 93d Cong., 1st sess. Washington, D. C.: U. S. Government Printing Office, 1973.

U. S. Congress. Senate. Committee on Labor and Public Welfare. Hearings on S. 1559 to Provide Assistance to Enable State and Local Governments to Assume Responsibility for Job Training and Community Service. Hearings before the Subcommittee on Employment, Poverty, and Migratory Labor, 93d Cong., 1st sess. Washington, D. C.: U. S. Government Printing Office, 1973.

U. S. Congress. Senate. Committee on Labor and Public Welfare. Implementing Comprehensive Manpower Legislation, 1974--Case Studies of Selected Manpower Programs. Prepared for the Subcommittee on Employment, Poverty, and Migratory Labor, 93d Cong., 2nd sess. Washington, D. C.: U. S. Government Printing Office, 1974.

U. S. Congress. Senate. Committee on Labor and Public Welfare. Report on S. 1559, the Job Training and Community Services Act of 1973. 93d Cong., 1st sess. Washington, D. C.: U. S. Government Printing Office, 1973.

U. S. Department of Labor. "Regulations for Comprehensive Manpower Programs and Grants to High Unemployment Areas." Federal Register 40:22674, 1975.

U. S. Department of Labor. Manpower Administration.
Interchange beginning June 1974.

U. S. Department of Labor, Manpower Administration.
Manpower Report of the President 1971-1975.
Washington, D. C. : U. S. Department of Labor 1971-
1975.

U. S. Department of Labor. Manpower Administration.
Technical Assistance Guides for Prime Sponsors under
the Comprehensive Employment and Training Act of
1973. Washington, D. C. : U. S. Department of Labor.

> Apprenticeship and CETA, 1974.
> CETA Coordination with WIN, 1974.
> CETA/SESA Guide, 1975.
> Community Based Organizations, 1974.
> Equal Employment Opportunity, 1974.
> Fiscal Activities Guide, 1974.
> Forms Preparation Handbook, 1974.
> Management Informations Systems Guide, 1974.
> Manpower Program Planning Guide, 1974.
> Organization and Staffing Guide, 1974.
> Program Activities and Services Guide, 1974.
> Program Assessment Guide, 1974.

U. S. Office of Management and Budget. Special
Analyses--Budget of the United States Government,
Fiscal Year 1976. Washington, D. C. : U. S. Govern-
ment Printing Office, 1975.

Wetzel, James R. and Martin Ziegler. "Measuring
Unemployment in States and Local Areas." Monthly
Labor Review. 97(6):40-46, 1974.

RELATED MATERIALS

Advisory Committee to the Department of Housing and Urban Development. Revenue Sharing and the Planning Process--Shifting the Locus of Responsibility for Domestic Problem Solving. Washington, D. C.: National Academy of Sciences, 1974.

Goss, Robert P. "State Manpower Services Councils, Promises--Problems--Progress." Washington, D. C.: 1975 National Governors' Conference, Center for Policy Research and Analysis, 1975.

Goetz, Charles J. What is Revenue Sharing? Washington, D. C.: The Urban Institute, 1972.

Levitan, Sar A. and Robert Taggart. "Employment and Earnings Inadequacy: A New Social Indicator." Challenge, 16:22-29, 1974.

Marshall, Patricia. "Paving the Way for Local Control." Manpower 6(4):2-9, 1974.

Mogulof, Melvin B. Special Revenue Sharing in Support of the Public Social Services. Urban Institute paper. Washington, D. C.: Urban Institute, 1973.

Nathan, Richard P., Allen D. Manvel and Susannah E. Calkins. Monitoring Revenue Sharing. Washington, D. C.: The Brookings Institution, 1975.

National League of Cities/U. S. Conference of Mayors. Manpower Reorganization and the Cities Vol. 2. Washington, D. C.: National League of Cities/U. S. Conference of Mayors, 1974.